Nose Art

Nose Art

80 YEARS OF AVIATION ARTWORK

J. P. Wood

BARNES
&NOBLE
BOOKS
NEW YORK

This edition published by Barnes & Noble, Inc.,
by arrangement with Salamander Books Ltd.

1999 Barnes & Noble Books

M1098765432

ISBN 0-7607-1488-6

All correspondence concerning the content of this volume should be
addressed to Salamander Books Ltd.

Editorial and design: Brown Packaging Ltd.

Colour Reproduction: Colour Systems, Kent.

Printed and bound in Italy

Page 1: An A-10 Warthog tankbuster shows off its fearsome profile for the camera (Austin Brown Aviation Picture Library).
Pages 2–3: A fine display of contemporary 'nose art' on a line-up of prop-driven fighters (Austin Brown Aviation Picture Library).
These pages: 'Amazing Andrea', a B-25 Mitchell, with World War II-style artwork (Austin Brown Aviation Picture Library).

CONTENTS

Airframe Art

The history of aircraft 'nose art' is as old as military aviation itself. From World War I to the 1991 Gulf War, pilots and ground staff have painted morale-boosting images on their charges, often in the face of official prohibition.

The fashion for decorating the tools of war with personal markings is as old as man himself, and as the machines of war developed in size and sophistication, so too did the decoration applied to them. It was perhaps at sea that this feature was most notable. The warships of all maritime nations in the age of sail were invariably decorated with an ornate figurehead on the bow, usually an idealised female sculpture, that was the pride of the crew and a good luck symbol. It doesn't take a great leap of imagination to see the common link between the sea-going figureheads and the painted 'pin-ups' on the metal skins of modern combat aircraft.

'Nose art' in World War I

World War I saw the deployment of the very first combat aircraft, but it was some time after their introduction into frontline service that crew members began to personalise their new weapons by painting images on the sides and front of their canvas-covered aircraft. At first, these machines were seen as somewhat bizarre curiosities and were treated with a certain reverence by both air and ground crews, a situation that often precluded the application of any personal markings. As the war progressed, however, aircraft became a much more common sight, and the first signs of 'art' began to appear on the fabric of these fragile flying machines. The most appropriate place for these early efforts was found to be the sides of the fuselage, either directly under the open cockpit cut-out or just aft of it. Simple graphic designs began to appear which clearly identified the occupant of the cockpit or the squadron he belonged to. Graphic devices, such as diamonds, hearts and circles, sometimes containing initials or slogans, were particularly popular. The size and nature of these first markings varied enormously from unit to unit and from country to country. As the war progressed the designs became more intricate and varied. The first recorded example of 'nose art' appeared in the shape of a lavish sea-monster painted on the nose of an Italian flying boat as early as 1913.

Left: This North American B-25 Mitchell medium bomber 'Big Bad Bonnie' displays a typical example of World War II 'nose art'. Note also the three 'kills', the tally of eight bombing missions and the names of some of the crew. The aircraft is, of course, an accurate replica.

Royal Flying Corps aircraft, possibly due to traditional British reserve, featured very few examples of outstanding or garish artwork. On the other hand, the French and the Italians, possibly in keeping with their supposedly more flamboyant national characteristics, produced some extremely colourful and attractive personal markings. The Germans, at least before the United States entered the war in 1917, certainly have to be considered the most avid exponents of individual aircraft artwork. They developed

Below: A modern re-creation of one of World War I's most famous planes — the predominantly red Fokker D VII scout flown by German ace Ernst Udet. The name of the aircraft — 'LO!' — is a reference to Udet's wife. The idea of individual emblems perhaps harks back to the knights of old.

the form in World War I to such an extent that crew members applying personal markings to aircraft today still use the style of German artwork as a guide and as inspiration. Manfred von Richtofen's squadron became known around the world as the 'Flying Circus', a name reflecting the variety of colours and designs painted onto its aircraft. When the Americans arrived in Europe during the war's final stages, they adopted the German fashion of decorating their combat aircraft with extremely bright individualised colour schemes.

It was also the Germans, late in World War I, who initiated the tradition of decorating their aircraft with the addition of a painted mouth under the propeller spinner on the nose of some appropriately shaped aircraft. Technically, this can probably be described as the first 'nose art'

as it was applied to the front rather than the side of the machine. Until this time most other personal markings had been positioned in the middle of the fuselage or, more unusually, covering the whole aircraft. Richtofen's all-red fighter and Hermann Goering's all-white Fokker D VII were fairly typical of this type of decoration.

Black horses and coloured patterns

One interesting case study of the development of an individual's personal aircraft markings concerns that of the rampant black horse painted on the side of Francesco Baracca's SPAD XIII in World War I. Baracca was one of Italy's greatest aces and the late Enzo Ferrari's brother had served and died in the same squadron. As is well known, Enzo Ferrari became involved in motor

racing after the war and he is reputed to have paid Baracca's family a visit, asking if he could integrate the now-legendary black horse into his racing team's shield. His request was, of course, granted. Today, Baracca's personal emblem also forms the basis for the unit insignia of the Italian

Right: *A French Caudron bomber from World War I with an impish figure in red and black carrying a white wand (or bomb).*

Below: *This Fokker D VII carries the distinctive and macabre colours of a World War I ace. Symbols of mortality, as in the case of this 'death's head', have always been a common motif in 'nose art' and, given the short combat life of many pilots in World War I, was entirely appropriate. The saying on the aircraft's tail, 'Du doch nicht', translates as 'You, not a chance'.*

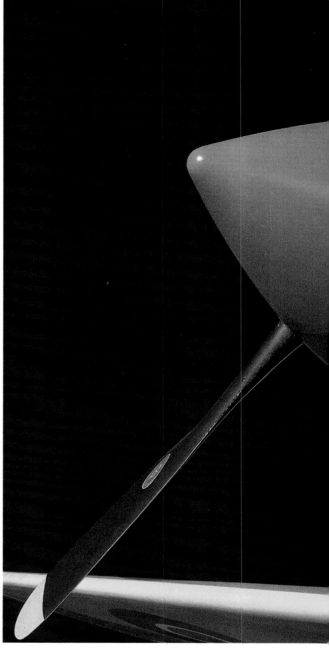

Above left: A World War II Italian bomber crew stand next to a classic piece of 'nose art' — a villainous cartoon character complete with eye patch and six-shooter. 'La Torrida' means 'The Hot One'.

Above: An example of perhaps the most common type of aircraft artistry — the sharksmouth. Here, a P-40 Tomahawk of No 112 Squadron, dressed in desert camouflage, bares its fangs. This design was the inspiration for the famous 'Flying Tigers'.

Left: Walt Disney's cartoon characters have always been a popular subject. This example of Donald Duck adorns the fuselage of a Spitfire with the RAF's No 303 (Polish) Squadron.

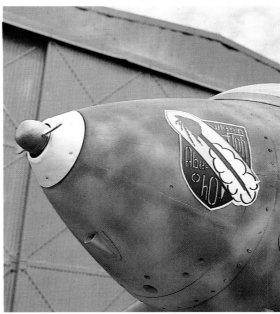

Above: *This Luftwaffe Me 163 Komet carries an apt motto: 'Wie ein floh — aber Oh-ho' ('Only a flea, but Oh-ho'). Its small size belied its performance: a climb rate of 16,000ft (4900m) per minute, a speed of 600mph (960km/hr) and a fearsome array of cannon.*

while developing a competent indigenous aviation industry. Germany had been forced to develop its Luftwaffe in secret, limited by the rules of the Treaty of Versailles signed at the end of World War I. All of the military aircraft produced were painted in bogus civil schemes to get round the treaty. Even in the USA there was no great interest in painting individual markings on either army or navy aircraft. Although, in a similar scheme to that of the RAF, the US Navy had developed an intricate scheme of very colourful identification markings, it wasn't until the outbreak of the Spanish Civil War in 1936 that fighting men were to resume the painting of 'nose art' to any extent.

Defying orders and regulations

It is clear that the 'nose art' phenomenon seems to reach its greatest extent during times of war and it would appear that the underlying causes behind the appearance of individual markings on warplanes are psychological in nature. Most participants in a war cannot help but be aware of the possibility of their death in combat. It is my personal conviction that this brutal reality gives an airman or soldier a tendency to flout the authority – at least to some extent – that has placed him in such a precarious position. During peacetime, professional soldiers abhor any deviation from established regulations as this tends to have negative effects on their 'career

Air Force's 10th Fighter Squadron (X Stormo Caccia) which flies F-104 Starfighters.

The end of World War I saw a dramatic reduction in the size of the military forces around the globe and a corresponding drop in the total number of combat aircraft. While this period of aviation history between the wars is commonly known as 'The Golden Years', it did not generate any 'nose art' of any significance. Most nations did, however, develop some very colourful paint schemes and unit insignia for their aircraft. Fighter squadrons in the Royal Air Force, for example, instituted a complex system of coloured individual geometric patterns,

loosely based on a more primitive system used in World War I, to identify individual squadrons. Personal markings were generally limited to the rank pennants of senior officers.

Elsewhere in Europe, however, brighter markings were far more common. In France, very colourful squadron insignia, some based on the personal markings of individual aces, continued to be applied to the temporarily idle combat aircraft. Italian aviators managed to reach something of a high point by producing hundreds of colour schemes for their combat machines. Similarly, the Polish Air Force developed some quite brightly coloured aircraft

potential'. During both world wars, the greater part of every nation's armed forces consisted of citizen soldiers who had no desire to continue a military career after the end of the conflict. It may have been, therefore, that they were less likely to adhere to regulations.

The generals and admirals who have been responsible for outlining the rules that govern the painting of official markings on aircraft have never accepted a need for 'nose art'. Usually, it is merely tolerated rather than approved. Senior officers are more concerned with detailing the official camouflage colours and regulation recognition devices for their aircraft. The phenomenon of 'nose art' usually, though not exclusively, appears 'in the field', under war conditions and in locations that are often well away from the 'eyes' of higher headquarters. Obviously, some services or units tend to have a tighter grip on their men than others, but an individual's urge to personalise his fighting machine is likely to be ultimately more important to the existence or absence of 'nose art' than rules and regulations.

During the Spanish Civil War (1936-39), many examples of personalised markings appeared on the fuselage sides of combat aircraft. Well-known cartoon characters such as Mickey Mouse and Popeye were used to decorate aircraft on both the Republican and the Nationalist sides. There were also quite a number of aircraft that were marked with political slogans and baser graffiti, some examples of which are too rude to print.

The 'Golden Age' of 'nose art'

In World War II, during the time between Germany's conquest of Poland (September 1939) and the invasion of France (May 1940), the combat aircraft of both sides displayed drab camouflage schemes and personal markings were notably absent. The Germans created the first 'nose art' in the shape of the traditional squadron shields that were painted on both fighter and bomber aircraft. These were officially designed and approved emblems that were applied to

Above left: The preserved B-17 Flying Fortress *'Virgin's Delight'* shows off its colours. One World War II namesake, flying with the Eighth Air Force's 94th Bombardment Group from England, was lost over Germany on 30 November 1943.
Left: Elmer Fudd, invariably the fall guy to the much smarter Bugs Bunny, offers a wave and a smile from the nose of a USAAF B-17. His hunting rifle at least suggests a more aggressive nature. This particular Flying Fortress does, however, have a very impressive number of missions to its credit, some of which are just visible. Mission tallies were often a good indication of the skill of the aircrew — or their luck in action.

aircraft as they arrived at the front, and were used throughout the war as a recognition device, though, no doubt, they did play a part in maintaining unit cohesion and morale.

While it is clearly impossible to determine the precise date that the first example of 'nose art' appeared on aircraft stationed either side of the English Channel, it probably occurred on the Luftwaffe's side, if only because of its pilots misplaced confidence about the final outcome of the impending Battle of Britain. German morale

....

Right: *Scantily clad or naked women have always been the most popular form of 'nose art'. This B-17 'Sally B' displays a well-executed example of the genre.*

Below right: *The crew of 'Tom Paine', a B-17 attached to the Eighth Air Force's 388th Bombardment Group, prepare for a mission. The motto, 'Tyranny, like Hell, is not easily Conquered!', is taken from Paine's political writings that were popular during the American Revolution.*

Below: *'Idiot's Delight', a B-17 of the 94th Bombardment Group, displays an impressive, if chaotic, operational tally.*

Left: A revealing close-up of the Flying Fortress 'Miss Barbara' that was attached to the 305th Bombardment Group in Europe during 1943. Many of these figures were inspired by artwork that appeared in such magazines as Esquire which were readily available to servicemen worldwide.

Below left: A much simpler form of artwork is shown on this B-17 'Hannah'. Official disapproval may have curtailed more expressive designs featuring naked or semi-clad figures.

was probably at its highest point of the war following the lightning conquest of Europe. One of the most notable personal markings was that of General Adolf Galland, who was a fighter squadron commander in 1939. Several of the Messerschmitt Bf109 fighters assigned to him carried his personal emblem of a gun-toting, cigar-smoking Mickey Mouse beneath the cockpit. This emblem was also applied to the fighter he flew during the Spanish Civil War. The practice of painting a small personal emblem under the cockpit of fighters was fairly widespread in the Luftwaffe at this time, although it seems to have been a privilege mainly reserved for the higher-scoring aces.

On the other side of the Channel, during the desperate days before the Battle of Britain, British airmen were more concerned with the defence of their nation than with decorating their fighting machines with personal markings. As the air battle progressed and confidence grew, aircrews began to apply some modest designs to their mounts. Again, it was the high-scoring fighter pilots that first began to apply 'kill' markings, usually small swastikas under the cockpit, to keep score. Some early examples of rather modest 'nose art' slowly began to appear alongside the 'scorecards'. Examples include a Hurricane MkI, code JX-B, flown by Flying Officer A.V. Clowes which had a colourful wasp under the engine exhaust, while the redoubtable Squadron Leader D.R.S. Bader's Hurricane had a painting in the same position depicting a boot kicking Hitler in the seat of his trousers.

Top right: 'Nose art' was never as widespread or dramatic in the Royal Air Force during World War II as it was in its American counterpart. This B-25 Mitchell twin-engined medium bomber 'Nulli Secundus' ('Second to None') is also decorated with a traditional red lion.

Above right: One of Walt Disney's Seven Dwarfs — 'Grumpy' — is displayed on this modern copy of a North American B-25 Mitchell. Disney took an active interest in creating new designs and unit insignia for wartime artists.

Right: 'Miami Clipper' displays all the essentials of classic 'nose art' — a bikini-clad, alluring woman lounging against an exotic background, in this case a desert island.

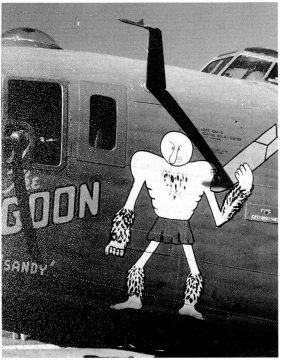

Above: *This B-25 'Bedsheet Bomber' artwork is clearly inspired by the work of Peruvian-born artist Alberto Vargas, who published his famous female pin-ups in* Esquire *during the 1940s and* Playboy *in the 1960s.*

Left: *The Consolidated B-24 Liberator 'The Goon' shows a much cruder form of 'nose art'. Also of interest is the nickname of crew member 'Sandy' displayed under the cockpit and to the left of the figure. The quality of artwork depended on the standards of local artists, either men serving with the squadron or a civilian.*

After the Battle of Britain had ended and the Japanese attack on Pearl Harbor (December 1941) had forced the United States into the fray, the US Eighth Air Force began to arrive at airfields in Britain, most notably in East Anglia. The Flying Fortresses and Thunderbolts initially arrived covered with drab green and grey camouflage, with few if any personal markings applied. Some of the bombers may have had nicknames painted on their noses, often acquired while they were assigned to training units on the other side of the Atlantic,

but the classic forms of 'nose art' were noticeably missing at this stage.

Farther away from 'home' and the high command, other units were developing unofficial symbols. In North Africa, for example, the RAF's No 112 Squadron had applied 'sharkmouths' to their US-built Curtiss Tomahawks. These ground-attack aircraft had a long pointed nose that lent itself to incorporating this fearsome image. No 112 Squadron's efforts inspired the American Volunteer Group (AVG), better known as the 'Flying Tigers', to paint similar mouths on their aircraft, also Tomahawks. Many of the 'Flying Tigers' aircraft were also decorated with personalised markings.

Cartoon strip characters go to war

One of the first US units in the European Theatre of Operations (ETO) to initiate an organised scheme of 'nose art' was the 56th Fighter Group. This unit had arrived in England in January 1943 and was equipped with brand new P-47C Thunderbolts. The first markings applied over the camouflage were white identification stripes painted on the tail grouping

and nose to avoiding confusion with the Luftwaffe's similar-looking Fw190s. The engine cowling of the Thunderbolt was quite large and provided an appropriate surface on which to apply personal markings. At first, the squadron attempted to maintain a theme of characters that inhabited the daily syndicated newspaper cartoon strip 'Li'l Abner' created by the satirist Al Capp. Li'l Abner, Daisy Mae, and Hairless Joe were just a few of colourful drawings that decorated the Thunderbolt cowlings. As an interesting aside, Al Capp had occasionally included a character within his comic strip called Fearless Fosdick who satirized the style of

Left: *A pugnacious eagle decorates the side of this fighter. The Eagle Squadrons consisted of American pilots who fought for the RAF before the United States entered World War II. Clearly, the eagle reflects the squadron name and its aggressive fighting spirit.*
Below: *A beautifully restored P-51 Mustang shows off its colours. Societies such as the Confederate Air Force in the United States regularly hold meetings to display these veteran aircraft.*

another contemporary comic character, Dick Tracy. The images of Fearless Fosdick and his arch enemy Evil Eye Fleagle were to adorn several aircraft as examples of 'nose art' in their own right. It wasn't very long before attempts at thematic illustration gave way to a complete 'free for all'. Halfway through World War II, 'nose art' was to enter a phase of development that has seen no historical parallel.

'Murder Incorporated'

Throughout the ETO, USAAF squadrons seemed to have been possessed by a passion to

Left: P-51 'LOU IV' returns to base 'somewhere in England' after escorting bombers over Germany. Note the long-range fuel tanks and black-and-white invasion stripes. It was common for pilots to take aircraft names with them. Presumably 'LOUs I, II and III' were previously flown by the same pilot.
Below: Cartoon villain Yosemite Sam covers the side of P-51 'Six-shooter'.

outdo each other, with bigger and better artwork appearing on the noses of every type of aircraft. As the war in Europe progressed and the Allies gained air superiority, the practice of painting 'nose art' on combat aircraft became almost mandatory and sometimes appeared to have run completely out of control. One example of this phenomenon was a B-26 Marauder crew who had unfortunately christened their medium bomber, not without some irony, 'Murder Incorporated'. Bomber crews inevitably identified with their aircraft and it was a common practice of the era to have the aircraft's name and artwork reproduced on the back of leather flying jackets. 'Murder Incorporated' had the misfortune to be shot down over Germany and, while the crew survived, they were captured. The Nazi propaganda machine, under a great deal of pressure to score a 'victory' to offset the demoralising effect of the constant bombing, was delighted to be presented with the opportunity to make a film depicting the captured airmen

with their painted jackets as 'Chicago Gangsters', dedicated to the destruction of the Third Reich. The film is alleged to have been shown throughout Hitler's Europe and actually caused the USAAF to order a review of all aircraft names.

'Nose art' legends

One work of 'nose art' that actually achieved worldwide fame in a propaganda short and, more recently, in a feature film was that of the famous Flying Fortress 'Memphis Belle'. In World War II, the experiences of its crew were recorded by

Right: The 'nose art' of US ace Don Gentile's P-51 Mustang — a battling eagle and the lettering 'Shangri-La', the mythical valley of plenty and tranquillity. The aircraft also had an impressive 'kill' tally.
Below: A voluptuous blonde reclines along the forward fuselage of the P-51 'Passion Wagon', a restored warbird of the Confederate Air Force.

Right: *This B-29 Superfortress 'Lucky 'Leven' of the 498th Bombardment Group certainly lived up to its name, flying 60 missions over Japan between November 1944 and August 1945. Unsurprisingly, lucky charms (four-leaf clovers, horseshoes and the like) remain a common form of aircraft 'nose art'. A combination of skill and luck were, and are, needed to survive the dangers of combat flying.*

Below right: *Port view of the P-38 Lightning 'Lander 3715'. This aircraft, attached to the USAAF 18th Fighter Group, flew out from bases in New Guinea from August 1944 to attack Japanese targets in Borneo and the Philippines. The reclining, scantily clad figure is based on a Vargas illustration.*

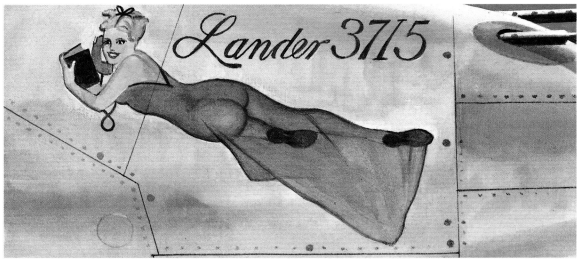

William Wyler on their twenty-fifth and final mission. The footage was used to promote War Bonds. A second (feature) film was made in the late 1980s.

Another piece of 'nose art' featured prominently in the plot of a film made just after the war, 'Twelve O'Clock High'. The fictitious story featured a Flying Fortress called 'The Leper Colony' to which the group commander, played by Gregory Peck, assigned cowardly aircrew. It is not known whether this procedure was actually followed during the war but it is unlikely. One reason for doubts is that the film reinforces the false assumption that aircrews actually flew the same aircraft on every mission. This was certainly not the case, as there were many more crews assigned to squadrons than aircraft. This remains normal military practice and, while the senior crews did have their own names and 'nose art' applied to their specific aircraft, the less senior crews flew them as well.

Nicknames and dragons

As the war ground on the RAF seems to have caught the 'nose art' bug from the USAAF. Bomber Command appears to have relaxed its tight control and, at squadron level, air and ground crews adopted the American fashion of applying garish paintings to the noses of their Lancaster and Halifax bombers. Two notable examples were the Halifax BVII, PN230, EQ-V, 'Vicky', which had an appropriate pin-up, and the Lancaster BI, RF141, JO-U, 'Uncle Joe Again', with a portrait of Joseph Stalin on a red flag. Fighter Command on the other hand was still loathed to adopt the fashion. The most dramatic deviation from regulation colours that had official approval was the alteration of standard unit and aircraft code letters on either side of the fuselage roundels to the initials of high ranking officers. The 'D-B' on Douglas Bader's aircraft was a good example of this practice. Pilots of Europe's occupied nations flying with the RAF were permitted to paint small national flags on the noses of their Spitfires, Hurricanes and Typhoons which added

a touch of additional colour to the normally drab camouflage schemes.

England, above all, has a literary heritage and this characteristic was sometimes reflected in the type of graffiti that appeared on the noses of RAF flying machines. Two such examples were Lancaster BI, R5868, PO-S, with one of Hermann Goering's less fortunate quotes lettered on its nose: 'No enemy plane will fly over the Reich territory'. Although a bit verbose for an aircraft nickname, its superb irony cannot be ignored: there are 98 mission markers neatly painted above the quote that belie the pompous boast of the Reich Marshal. The Lancaster is now on display at the RAF Museum at Hendon. The other was a Typhoon IB, RB222, TP-F, on which the pilot had painted on the engine cowling: 'If this engine catches fire on starting, don't just wave your arms at the pilot, try putting the bloody thing out as well'. This long bit of

prose would seem to indicate a certain lack of confidence on the pilot's behalf regarding the competence of the ground crew to cope with emergencies. On the other side of the nose was a short verse: 'If fate decrees that I should fail, then fate will not have watched my tail'. One wonders if his wingman was named 'Fate' and, if so, how much the pilot trusted his abilities.

Back in the airfields of 'Little America', as the USAAF bases in England were called, when victory over the Germans seemed more or less assured, camouflage was no longer applied to combat aircraft and 'nose art' scaled new heights. The aircrews felt little or no inhibition when taking brush in hand to decorate their mounts. At the time of the collapse of the Third Reich, the Allies were regrouping to end the war in the Pacific. The troops already involved in the war against the Imperial Japanese forces had themselves been experimenting with the now

well-established traditions of 'nose art'. While the best examples of the genre in the ETO were applied to B-17 Flying Fortresses, on the tiny islands and atolls in the Pacific where the USAAF bombers were based, art was applied to B-24 Liberators and, later, B-29 Superfortresses.

It was on these remote island airfields that the form truly began to get out of hand. 'Nose art' began to grow in size until entire aircraft were decorated from nose to tail. The most conspicuous example of this was a Liberator named 'The Dragon and his Tail'. This aircraft depicted a huge green dragon with a 'fair damsel' gripped in its claws. Its tail extended all the way down the fuselage of the large bomber to the tailplane. Superfortresses further refined the quality of the 'nose art' and few people will ever forget the most famous of these, 'Enola Gay' and 'Bocks Car', which delivered the atomic bombs to Hiroshima and Nagasaki. Both

of these aircraft and their 'nose art' are preserved in the United States today.

Other countries involved in World War II did not produce 'nose art' on the scale of the USAAF, the RAF and Commonwealth Air Forces. The USSR did decorate combat aircraft with 'kill markings' and political slogans, but it is apparent that the fashion for embellishment was not really adopted by that country. The Japanese avoided such expressions of individuality. However, towards the end of the war, some individual markings did begin to appear on aircraft, particularly on those of high-scoring pilot aces.

The Korean War
When the war ended, the United States was eager to disarm, and thousands of aircraft were ferried back to be temporarily stored in the huge aircraft graveyards in the state of Arizona.

Above: 'Raz'n Hell', a name referring either to the Superfortress's role as a long-range heavy bomber in World War II and the Korean War or the intention of the crew to let their hair down after a mission. Either way, a devilish, scantily clad siren with horns and forked tail riding a falling bomb covers both possible angles.

Countless others were scrapped where they were based around the world. The proud mounts of many aircrew ended their days sitting in the dry desert awaiting the breaker. Many, with their excellent examples of 'nose art' gradually fading in the hot sun, would have escaped the eyes of future historians were it not for the efforts of some forward-thinking workers who could not bring themselves to destroy this art. Many examples of quality 'nose art' were cut from the aircraft prior to scrapping and dozens of these delightful aluminium panels are now on display

Above: *The ample nose of the B-29 Superfortress provided plenty of scope for large-scale artwork. 'It's Hawg Wild', seen here undergoing complete restoration, is no exception.*

Left: *The crew of B-29 'Mission Inn' clearly understood the role of strategic bombing during the Korean War (1950-53) — to drive the North Korean armed forces back beyond the 38th Parallel, the line that divided that country from South Korea. 'Mission Inn' served with the USAF's 22nd and 19th Bombardment Groups during the conflict. Many of the B-29s deployed during the conflict were veterans of the great raids against Japan in World War II.*

at the Confederate Air Force Museum in Texas.

While World War II is quite rightly regarded as the 'Golden Age' of aircraft 'nose art', the end of the conflict did not signal the demise of the art. The practice managed to survive the short peace between 1945 and the Korean War (1950-53). The aircraft that remained within the borders of the two defeated Axis powers as a part of the occupation forces continued to display their flamboyant markings. Even back in the USA, the USAF reserve squadrons and Air National Guard (ANG) units still continued the tradition, albeit in a somewhat subdued fashion. In the UK the phenomenon virtually vanished, with official squadron badges adding the only colour to the traditional national insignia.

When the North Korean Army crossed the 38th Parallel to invade South Korea in 1950, the aircraft of the USAF based in the Far East formed the heart of the UN air force, and most of the World War II vintage aircraft in place had colourful 'nose art' already applied. The most modern post-war type, the F-82 Twin Mustang, formed the basis of the all-weather fighter defence and many of these had very colourful examples of personal markings applied over their all-black paint schemes. As the war intensified and the number and variety of UN combat aircraft dramatically increased, so too did the

Right: *'Flying Stud II' carries the full panoply of typical 'nose art' including a dragon and an impressive number of mission and 'kill' markings. The significance of the camel silhouettes is not immediately apparent; in fact they refer to sorties over the 'Hump' between India and China.*
Below: *A Vought F-8 Crusader bares its teeth as it leaves the USS* Oriskany *for a raid on North Vietnam.*

'nose art' applied to them. The North Koreans and their allies, the Chinese, continued the orthodox communist policy of omitting personal markings from their combat aircraft. The introduction of modern jet aircraft into the conflict, particularly the F-86 Sabre, was to prove a particularly fertile medium for the art. Some of the most inspiring and outstanding examples of 'nose art' were to appear on the noses of this superior fighter.

When the USAF started the strategic bombing campaign against North Korea, it did so with ex-World War II B-29s based in Japan. These old warhorses continued the tradition of colourful markings that had been used while they were formerly deployed on the Pacific island bases five years earlier against the nation in which they were now stationed. It should not go without notice that the less spectacular tactical bombers, the B-26 Invaders, also displayed some excellent examples of well-done 'nose art'.

Sharksmouths over Vietnam

After the end of the Korean War, there was a long period that saw 'nose art' disappear from most aircraft. It was more or less replaced by a system of bright colour schemes that would clearly identify individual squadrons or air groups. Pilots continued to have their names and rank painted on the canopy frame or elsewhere in the canopy area as a symbol of status. Some squadrons applied coloured stripes to the aircraft to denote flight leaders or commanding officers.

The advent of the war in Vietnam stimulated a new interest in 'nose art' that, while not reaching the standards set in World War II, was

Above right: *There's no mistaking this aircraft's wartime role of submarine hunter-killer. The aircraft in question is an RAF Shackleton long-range maritime reconnaissance aircraft. The cat is clearly inspired by the character of Tom from the 'Tom and Jerry' cartoon series.*
Above, far right: *The A-10's nose seems to cry out for a vicious pair of jaws. In this case, the tusks of a wild boar sprout from a tightly closed mouth.*
Right: *Possibly a case of overkill! A Fiat G-91 of the Portuguese Air Force attends one of the frequent 'Tiger Meets' held in Europe. A respray might be in order at a later date. Ferocious members of the animal world, particularly tigers, are a very popular form of art on fighters, though they do appear on all types of military aircraft.*

Above: One of the most popular subjects for 'nose art' has to be wise-cracking Bugs Bunny, usually with his punchline of 'What's up Doc?'. Here, a reclining Bugs grasps a bomb on the side of a Strategic Air Command Stratofortress which completed eight bombing missions in the 1991 Gulf War.

Right: 'Rip'n Tear', an A-10 of the 23rd Tactical Fighter Wing which played a prominent role in the war against Iraq. Much of this art was later removed when these units left the Gulf and returned to the United States.

quite impressive. When the war was still seen as a 'counter-insurgency' action, the aircraft present were all propeller-driven types in South Vietnamese Air Force (RVNAF) national markings, though piloted by USAF aircrew. The paint schemes and insignia of the T-28s, B-26s, and A-1 Skyraiders were all based on official US specifications. As the USAF was involved in an almost undeclared war which dictated that the US 'adviser' pilots play down their contribution, there was little opportunity to individually 'personalise' the aircraft involved.

When the war escalated and the Geneva Convention rule limiting the ratio of jet combat aircraft to propeller types was ignored, the USAF introduced its frontline jet aircraft to the

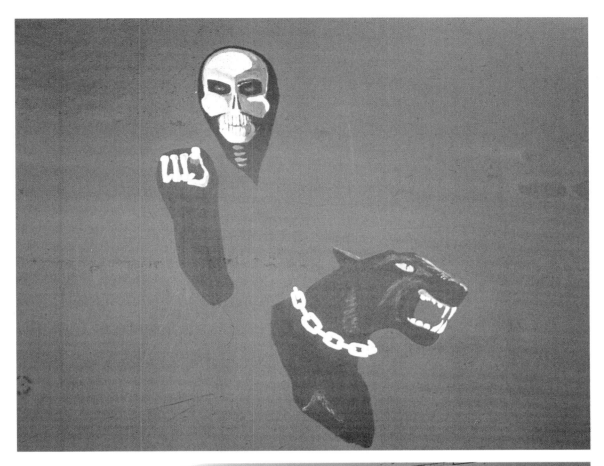

fray. At first these types arrived on station in the natural metal schemes that were then standard. As a humorous historical footnote, it is worthwhile to point out that the arrival of one F-105 Thunderchief squadron at a base in Thailand nearly caused an international incident. The aircraft in question arrived on the tarmac of the hot jungle air base resplendently decorated with 'sharksmouths', a traditional emblem in the unit, painted on all their noses. Apparently none of the personnel of the squadron was very well-read in recent history. If anyone had been, they would have had the 'sharksmouth' markings removed before their arrival, as the Thais were allies of the Japanese during World War II and they had fought against the AVG's P-40 Tomahawks which were also adorned with the legendary 'sharksmouths'. This fact was quickly pointed out to the American airmen, who had the offensive markings rapidly removed from all the aircraft.

A similar event occurred just after World War II, when Colonel Dave Schilling's squadron arrived in Europe after a trans-Atlantic ferry flight. Schilling's F-80 carrying his personal scorecard of German 'kill' markings painted on the nose. This would certainly have been seen as offensive to NATO's new German partners so they were equally quickly removed. As a former fighter pilot, it is the author's opinion that this was less an oversight than a failure of a major fighter ace's ability to alter a previous strongly held but understandable attitude.

Women, cartoons and graffiti

Before the USAF adopted the practice of camouflaging their warplanes in what is now known as the 'Southeast Asia' scheme, the all-metal aircraft began to acquire names which were followed by some modest 'nose art'. The arrival of camouflage initially led to their removal due to over-painting. Gaudy images displayed over drab-coloured paint defeated the purpose of camouflage. In fact, they were seen as being potentially dangerous and were discouraged for a time. The first signs of yet another revival of 'nose art' began with names and paintings rendered in dark red paint applied over the tan

Above left: *A design probably completed by the artist responsible for the work on the A-10 'Rip'n Tear' (bottom left). Certainly, the images and style are similar. Often, artistically minded squadron members paint a series of aircraft — a simple way of giving a unit a single identity.*

Left: *'Miss Liberty II', a USAF F-111 stationed at Lakenheath, England, has a distinguished record, taking part in the raid on Libya (April 1986) and leading the first raids on Iraq (January 1991). The imagery of woman, home and freedom are classic 'nose art' subjects.*

and greens of the official colour scheme. The matt red colour was essentially neutral in nature and the offending artwork couldn't be recognised even a short distance from the aircraft. The spirit and enterprise of the participating aircrew eventually could not be controlled by those in authority and 'nose art' proliferated once again. The attitude of the airmen could best be illustrated by the rhetorical question often expressed in the face of authority, 'What are you gonna' do, send me to Vietnam?'. Virtually all of the aircraft types that participated in the war displayed most of the varieties of the now traditional art, including the RVNAF aircraft. The North Vietnamese continued with

Right: Bugs Bunny takes on a more menacing image on the side of this USAF B-52 of the 2nd Bombardment Wing.
Below: A USAF KC-135 tanker 'Keystone Lady' of the Pennsylvania Air Guard. Pennsylvania is known as the 'Keystone State'. Again, a typical piece of art reflecting 'home and heart'. This tanker was operating in the build-up to 'Desert Storm'.

the policy of not permitting individual art save for some 'kill' markings displayed by their higher scoring aces on the noses of their MiG fighters.

Overall, the categories of art remained the same as in World War II and Korea (women, slogans, cartoons and graffiti) but some changes did occur due mostly to changing fashion. Most notably, cartoon figures took on a much more contemporary flavour, incorporating cartoonist Charles Schultz's 'Peanuts' characters Snoopy and Charlie Brown. It may seem curious that Andy Capp, a character created in Britain, also appeared on several USAF aircraft but, in fact, by this time he was syndicated in many US newspapers. The end of the war once again saw the curtailment of 'nose art', but many examples began to emerge in the early 1980s in Air National Guard squadrons. Some of these squadrons were receiving veteran Phantoms and Corsair IIs that had served in Vietnam and were delivered still proudly carrying the typical red star 'kill' markings which were applied during combat. Almost all of these were retained throughout the aircraft's career.

Official 'nose art'

In the late 1980s, Strategic Air Command (SAC) actually authorised the application of 'nose art' to its bomber and tanker aircraft. According to a directive the art applied should be in 'good taste'

and/or in a 'historical context' which meant that some of the original artwork created during World War II was to reappear on the noses of B-52s and KC-135s. In this new formalised form, art was generally displayed in smaller format and therefore was less spectacular visually, but it did add a degree of individuality to the normally dull paint schemes applied to SAC aircraft.

Generally, however, 'nose art' declined in popularity during the years between the Vietnam War and the outbreak of the Gulf War

in 1991. Even though the war in the Gulf was to last for only 100 days, there was a great revival of classic 'nose art' which came as a great surprise to many and a shock to others. The traditional standard bearers of 'nose art', the men of the USAF, were to find their admirable efforts completely overshadowed by the usually more subdued British. For some inexplicable reason, they pulled out all the stops to produce a genuinely dazzling array of painting on virtually all of their aircraft, both combat and support

Above left: Skilfully executed 'nose art' on the side of an RAF Victor K.2 tanker from No 55 Squadron deployed to support operations in the Gulf War. Six aircraft were deployed initially and each was given a similar paint job — with all of the women carrying a spear. Using similar images has always been seen as a way of creating a cohesive unit.
Above: Another of No 55 Squadron's tankers, 'Teasin' Tina'. The squadron, usually based at RAF Marham, completed nearly 300 refuelling sorties in the Gulf War.

types. Everything from the humble Hercules transports to the superb ground-attack Tornados carried the finest expressions of the air and ground crews' artistic abilities. Fortunately, despite a virtual press blackout on the grounds of military security, most of the artwork was dutifully recorded on film by the participants in the war.

The historical recording of the phenomenon parallels the pattern of the proliferation of

Far left: Cartoon character Garfield adorns the fuselage of an RAF Hercules transport in the Gulf. It was suggested that the slogan should have been changed to 'Life's a Beach'.
Left: Charles Schultz's cartoon creations for the 'Peanuts' strip have always been popular subjects for aircraft. This RAF Hercules 'The Baron' has Snoopy (as a pilot) on its side.
Below: 'MiG Eater', an RAF GR.1 Tornado in Gulf colours. Its 'nose art' includes a sharksmouth, a 'cool-looking' shark and an impressive list of missions, including three JP233 runway-cratering raids, 14 laser-guided bomb missions and 23 conventional bomb sorties.

privately owned cameras. As Western society has improved its standards of living during the course of this turbulent century, more and more individuals have had the opportunity to own a camera. As many of the photographs in this volume have come from private sources, it is apparent that 'official' photographers were (and still are!) not particularly interested in recording this colourful story. Much credit must be given to the courage and tenacity of the individual picture-takers who, under sometimes extremely stressful circumstances and official adversity,

continue to collect the photos that form the basis of this work.

While camera ownership has been more widespread and technology improved, so too has film quality. Today, we all use colour film without giving it a passing thought. During

World War II it was something of an expensive novelty. The author hopes that books such as this one will inspire others to dig out old photos of 'nose art' so that they can be used to complete the story of this delightful and fascinating subject.

Right: A port-sided view of RAF Buccaneer 'Miss Jolly Roger' in the Gulf with a suitably swashbuckling motif.

Below: A view of an aircraft from the same unit. 'Hello Sailor' carries, like other Buccaneers in the Gulf', four types of 'nose art': a female figure and name, a second name (presumably one of the crew's girlfriends), the name of a brand of Scotch whisky and a mission tally. This particular aircraft (XX885) has a Russian An-12 to its credit (destroyed on the ground) as well as a number of laser-guided bomb raids.

GRAFFITI

RESCUE

Gulf Kill

In times of war, when fighting men are forced to come to terms with their own mortality, it seems entirely reasonable that they should want to express themselves in a harmless fashion. Therefore, it should come as no surprise that the practice of utilising flying machines as a medium for self-expression has been, and remains, a common practice. The graffiti that has been recorded almost invariably contains the components of the language and feelings of the time, and generally expresses the human condition quite succinctly, if not a little crudely. Aircraft themselves often receive affectionate, or sometimes less than affectionate, names that describe the general view of the aircrew who have judged the quality and effectiveness of the specific airframe which they have either flown or maintained.

'Turkeys' and 'Flying Whores'

In World War II some of the aircraft types that were less favoured by their crews were given unflattering epithets that occasionally appeared in print on their aluminium skins. The Germans were well aware of the less than desirable performance and handling qualities of the Ju87 'Stuka' and it was known as the 'Schwein' ('pig'). This possibly well-founded criticism made its way into the design of unit emblems that were applied to the type. In contrast, the Ju52 transport was frequently admired for its reliability and became known as the 'Tante Ju' ('Auntie Junkers'). Likewise, American pilots also had aircraft that were viewed with a great deal of suspicion, though many of these initial slurs were later found to be unjustified. In spite of the fact that it ended the war with an outstanding combat record, the B-26 Marauder was, in its early days, known as 'The Widow Maker', a name which has also been applied to many other military aircraft since 1945. This unfortunate name was given to the type because its high-performance wing made its landing speeds considerably higher than most of the other contemporary airframes. Many pilots were ill-prepared for this new design and many aircraft did indeed crash while landing. It was also unflatteringly known as 'The Flying Whore'

Left: There's no mistaking the war being fought by this Royal Air Force Tornado GR. 1 – the 1991 conflict against Iraq. 'Gulf Killer' sports 31 mission artworks as well as a nubile girl riding a large phallic laser-guided bomb.

Above: A fine piece of commemorative artwork as applied to the USAF KC-10 tanker 'The Spirit of Kitty Hawk' which celebrates the pioneering flight of the Wright brothers in 1903.

because its short wingspan 'provided no visible means of support'.

Sometimes individual aircraft were singled out for a particular type of graffiti because crews were quick to recognise that, perhaps surprisingly, almost all aircraft possess unique individual characteristics despite modern mass-production techniques. Most units have had, at one time or another, one or two aircraft that became known as 'Hangar Queens' because they seem to spend more time under shelter receiving maintenance than they did in the air. One such Republic P-47 'Thunderbolt' received the name of 'Repulsive Thunderbox' on its cowling. The Grumman TBF Avenger of World War II was known to many as the 'Turkey' and the connotations of that derogatory name remain

in today's language. Another excellent example of graffiti giving a certain attribute to an aircraft was to do with one of the more successful B-26s which was given the name of 'Flak Bait' because it had taken so many hits from enemy anti-aircraft weapons yet survived.

Women, warthogs and nicknames

In the author's own squadron, one of the 'Hangar Queens' was known as 'The Sick, Sick Whore' as the last three digits of its serial number were '664', an American version of Cockney rhyming slang! One of the more modern types that was not at first generally accepted by its aircrew was the General Dynamics F-111. Its initial reputation was undeserved and resulted from politicians

exercising far too much influence in the design and procurement of the aircraft. First of all, the F-111 is not actually a fighter despite its 'F' designation. It clearly should have been given a 'B' designation as its primary mission is to deliver bombs to a target. Strategic Air Command's (SAC's) F-111s were designated 'FB' in recognition of this fact but the aircraft retained the original 'F' as a concession to the politics of the day. When the first F-111s were allocated to the USAF's Tactical Air Command (TAC), their unpopularity was mainly due to the fact that the pilots assigned to flying them were making the transition from single-engined, single-seat fighters. After all, as the pilots of that era complained, 'How can you call an aeroplane with two seats, two engines, and a rotating beacon a fighter?' As a result of the pilots' reluctance to accept their new role of 'Bomber Jockeys' and the F-111's obvious shortcomings as a fighter, they nicknamed it the 'Edsel'. This was a derogatory reference to the contribution of the then Secretary of Defense, Robert MacNamara, formerly a Ford Motor Company executive, and his participation in two projects: the TFX 'Fighter' (which later became the F-111), and the financial disaster resulting from

Ford's introduction of a 'new' automobile, the Edsel. The pilots felt so strongly about the subject that some squadrons actually privately purchased Edsels, painted them in USAF colours and adopted them as squadron mascots. The F-111 was ultimately accepted as an outstanding bomber and was renamed the 'Aardvark' because of its long drooping nose.

Another aircraft that was to have its official name permanently altered was the Fairchild Republic A-10 'Thunderbolt II', a ground-attack aircraft named after the World War II P-47 fighter. Because of its rather unorthodox and ugly appearance – straight wings, with two engines mounted high on the fuselage just

forward of the tailplane – it was christened the 'Warthog'. This name came from an underground comic strip called 'Wonder Warthog' whose chief protagonist was an ugly, satirical character who parodied contemporary 'Super Heroes'. The name subsequently appeared on the noses of many A-10 aircraft.

Tactical 'fighter' pilots who fly the 'Warthog' do so with mixed emotions as its sheer size and unorthodox appearance are at odds with the

Below: A famous piece of 'nose art' – Charles Lindbergh's 1927 Atlantic-crossing 'Spirit of St. Louis'. St. Louis was the home of Ryan, the aircraft's manufacturer.

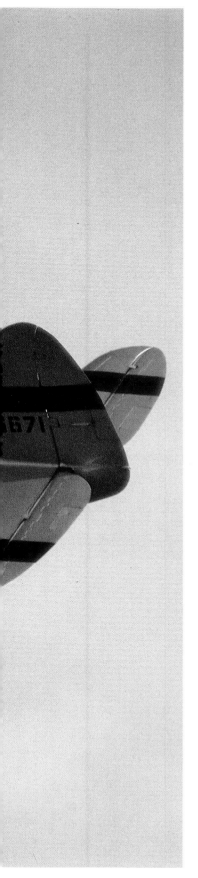

Above: 'Galloping Gertie', a fairly typical piece of war graffiti, which probably reflects the pilot's affection for his aircraft, appears on the side of this Bell P-63 Kingcobra. The fighter, with its unusual tricycle undercarriage, was not a success.

Left: A case of 'nose art' echoing down through the ages. This 'No Guts – No Glory' decoration appeared on a USAF F-105 Thunderchief in the early 1960s. The mouse contemplates air combat in an earlier age: World War I.

popular image of a typical sleek modern fighter. The general sentiment expressed about flying a 'Warthog' by its pilots is: 'It's a bit like self abuse. It's OK while you're doing it, but you don't like to boast about it.'

As ships all seem to be associated with the female gender, so do aircraft. The practice of applying women's names to warplanes is probably as old as the history of aviation itself and might now be considered a deep-seated tradition. Aircrew and ground crew alike appear to transfer that portion of their affection to their aircraft that they are unable to easily apply to their distant loved ones at home. Wives, daughters, girlfriends, and even mothers find their names affectionately applied to the noses of the most unlikely combat aircraft. The practice can be said to be universal as it appears on aircraft of all nations and all eras. One of the best examples was General Charles 'Chuck' Yeager's World War II P-51 Mustang 'Glamorous Glen', named after his wife Glennis. Several of Yeager's

Far left and left: A superb example of a World War II P-47 Thunderbolt long-range escort fighter in full warpaint – black-and-white chequered cowling, D-Day invasion stripes on wings and rear fuselage, two 'kill' marks and 'nose art' of 'No Guts – No Glory!'. The original aircraft was flown from Duxford, England, by Lieutenant Mayos of the USAAF's 78th Fighter Group during the latter part of World War II. 'Gung ho' graffiti has always been a common and popular form of artwork on fighters of all forces throughout aviation history.

subsequent Mustangs also had his wife's name, up to 'Glamorous Glen IV'. A less known fact is that the Bell X-1 experimental aircraft in which he was to be the first man to fly at supersonic speed also carried the name 'Glamorous Glennis' on its nose.

There have been several attempts by psychologists and academics to discover the underlying reasons for this 'personalisation' of aircraft, but all of the theories seem to fall short of the mark. If Freud was alive to add his opinion to the list, the results would probably be so complex as to obscure the simple truth that the males responsible for 'nose art' are only expressing a basic human need: to feel or record a part of 'normal' life.

While female names make up the greater part of this form of graffiti, the practice of giving

Above left: A fine example of fighter 'nose art' on this P-51 Mustang 'Double Trouble Two' with flying witch motif, possibly inspired by 'The Wizard of Oz'.
Top: 'Glamorous Jen', a P-51 Mustang complete with the almost obligatory scantily clad figure.
Above: A USAAF Mustang pictured 'somewhere in Europe' during the winter of 1944. 'Chihuahua' might refer to the Mexican city or, less likely, the short-haired and highly strung breed of dog.

the names of places to aircraft is also very common. Often the names on the noses of both USAAF and RAF aircraft would use the preface, 'The Spirit of....' to precede a place name. Occasionally, female names would combine with place names, such as 'Georgia Belle', a P-38 flown by fighter ace Captain Joel B. Paris. Another example was the P-51 Mustang named 'Janey Girl from Texas' piloted by Captain W.R. Yarborough. It would also seem perfectly normal for young men involved in a war far away from home to attach the names of their places of origin to their fighting machines and, indeed, the practice was widespread. 'Alabama Express', 'Arkansas Traveller', 'Michigan', 'Texas Doll', 'Texas Gal', and 'The Wichita Witch' are but a few of scores of examples.

Nicknames are quite a popular subject for 'nose art', and among the most notable examples

was the series of fighter aircraft flown by the now retired General Robin Olds. General Olds was a fighter pilot for his entire air force career, which began in Europe during World War II. All of his aircraft, the first a P-51 Mustang, were named 'Scat' and as the aircraft were replaced or updated, only the Roman numeral that followed the name was altered until his last aircraft, an F-4 Phantom flown during the Vietnam War, became 'Scat XXII'. There, he was to add an additional four MiGs downed to his World War II total of 13 'kills'.

Slogans, slang and challenges

Slogans and slang words, usually reflecting current social values and issues and expressed in modern terms, also form their own special category of aircraft graffiti. Some are relatively simple and straightforward and remain in

present-day usage, while the meanings of others may be lost forever due to their historical or national context. For example, 'Ski Nose and Handlebar' was a reference to the comedians Bob Hope and Jerry Collona, who were extremely popular with US servicemen during World War II, especially as both toured the war zones with the United Services Organisation (USO) shows. However, the name would mean little to today's pilots. It has been a long time since Bob Hope was called 'Ski Nose' by his former colleague, the equally famous singer Bing Crosby. The name 'Gremlin's Delight' would

Below: The North American B-25 Mitchell 'Georgia Girl' taxis down a runway prior to a demonstration flight. Naming aircraft after home states or the home of a girlfiend was common practice during World War II, and remains popular to this day.

Above: *The Martin B-26 Marauder medium bomber initially proved unpopular with flight crews due to high losses, often during landings. However, the Marauder had proved its worth and reliability by May 1945, being the aircraft with the lowest loss-rate of any US Army bomber in Europe.*

Left: *Possibly one of the most renowned B-26s of World War II, 'Mild and Bitter' served with the 322nd (Medium) Bombardment Group. It was the first B-26 to complete 100 missions and went on tour in the US covered with the autographs of 322nd Bombardment Group personnel.*

imply that the B-17 so named had recurrent maintenance problems. One cannot be absolutely sure whether another B-17 by the name of 'Dogs Breath' referred to the aircraft or one of its crew members, or perhaps even the crew's canine mascot!

Many of the slogans were thinly disguised puns on, or deliberate misspellings of, rude expressions. 'Shedonwanna', 'Lakanookie', and 'El Pistofo' need no further comment. A B-25 emblazoned with the name 'Poontang' might not have meant much to most British observers, but

Above: *The distinguished B-24 Liberator 'All American' commemorates members of the general public and other sponsors, including businesses, who have made donations to help pay for its upkeep and any repairs.*

Right: *A superb view of the nose of the RAF Lancaster bomber 'City of Lincoln'. The aircraft, which displays an impressive number of mission markings and is the only Lancaster still flying, is part of the RAF's Battle of Britain Memorial Flight.*

its sexual overtones might raise an eyebrow or two in the USA. There exists a theory among those who have made a study of the subject that the farther a military unit is based from its main headquarters the more outrageous the 'nose art' becomes. The RAF's experience in the Gulf War would seem to bear this out.

Graffiti on aircraft is by no means always simply names of some type or a rude slogan. During World War I, for example, a famous German ace had a 'dare', 'Du...doch nicht', written on the tailplane of his fighter which, roughly translated, means 'You – not a chance'. One cannot help but wonder how many Allied pilots would have understood the challenge had they the opportunity to read it. It would have certainly been more appropriate had it been printed in English or French. In modern warfare the enemy's only chance to read such challenges is if the appropriate part of the aircraft survives a crash on friendly territory. During World War I, however, it was the custom to land near the crash site of one's latest 'kill' and recover a piece of fabric, usually marked with the aircraft's serial number, to add to one's private collection. The rudders of German aircraft shot down over England or France during World War II were prized souvenirs for those who had the opportunity to get them. As the German aces traditionally applied their 'score' sheets and awards to the rudders of their fighters, these were much-valued acquisitions.

'Official' graffiti

Other forms of graffiti tend to appear on virtually every surface of combat aircraft. This was particularly true of World War II bombers, with each crew member happy to leave a trace of his identity near his crew position, usually painted on the outside of the aircraft. Gunners, navigators and the bombardier would frequently have their names and ranks neatly lettered close to their windows or turrets. When appropriate,

Top: 'Tabitha', a Northrop P-61 Black Widow, was attached to the USAAF's 442nd Night Fighter Squadron. The aircraft is pictured at its dispersal at Scorton, England, during autumn 1944. The all-black camouflage scheme reflects its wartime role.
Above: Probably the most famous piece of 'nose art' ever. 'Enola Gay', the B-29 Superfortress that dropped the first atomic bomb on Hiroshima (August 1945), was named after the mother of its commander, Colonel Paul Tibbets.
Left: 'Sentimental Journey', a B-29 Superfortress, was probably called after the popular Glen Miller song. Note also the name of two of the crew's girlfriends on the fuselage, close to the seating position of the appropriate flier.

individual 'kills' were also applied close to the nose in the shape of miniature Swastikas or Japanese flags. It was also not uncommon for multi-engined aircraft to receive individual names printed on each of the cowlings.

More ambitious graffiti often covered the whole wing or tail surfaces. At the end of World War II, one such example was a Mediterranean-based B-25 which had 'Finito Benoto, Next Hirohito' in large letters from wing tip to wing tip. Another classic was a USAF KC-135 tanker aircraft which had the inscription 'Kick Ass' painted on the undersurfaces of the tailplane to

Right: *A typical piece of basic 'nose art' appears on this F-100 Super Sabre 'Lethiferous Lola' which is being prepared at Phan Rang Air Base, South Vietnam, August 1970. Artwork during the Vietnam War was, in general, much more restrained than in previous conflicts, though sharksmouths retained their popularity with pilots.*

Below: *This B-47 Stratojet 'Spirit' was one of over 2000 such aircraft that formed the backbone of the USAF's medium bomber force during the 1950s.*

Above: *A fine close-up shot of the 410th Bombardment Wing's B-52 'Someplace Special'. Someplace special could be the unit's home in Michigan, K.I. Sawyer Air Force Base. Many B-52s carried outlines of states where they are normally based during the Gulf War against Iraq.*

Left: *A case of art imitating life, perhaps? Certainly the nose of this Fairchild C-82 Packet 'Nose for News' is more than big enough to accommodate any large-scale artwork applied to it.*

inspire all of its customers during the 1991 Gulf War. One of the least expected of these classic excesses, 'Desert Storm', was painted atop the wing of a US Navy A-7 Corsair II. The US Navy has traditionally and consistently frowned upon the use of personalised markings on its aircraft.

Some examples of more 'official' graffiti appear on military aircraft at the time a particular model leaves the factory production line. One type of official 'nose art' has been around for a considerable time and examples of it can still be found on modern aircraft. Production milestones are much photographed for publicity purposes

Left: The General Dynamics, Grumman-modified EF-111A tactical electronic countermeasures aircraft 'Let'em Eat Crow'. The lightning shooting from the crow's foot reflects its battlefield role of masking enemy radar systems, thereby allowing attack aircraft to get through to their targets.
Below and bottom left: Two examples of the USAF's F-111 strategic attack bomber – 'June Night' and 'Cherry Bomb'. Together, the names reflect two of the aircraft's great features: a large payload and superb night-flying abilities. F-111s flew from Turkey to attack targets in Iraq during the 1991 Gulf War.

and have large letters, such as '5000th Phantom', painted on the nose in bold, colourful characters. As a rule these gaudy markings are removed before the aircraft is formally delivered to the military. As a case in point, the '5000th Phantom' was actually delivered to the South Korean Air Force in a two-tone grey camouflage scheme that was completely different from the ceremonial blue and white one it sported during the ceremony to mark its completion.

Manufacturers' graffiti

During World War II there were countless such aircraft production milestones as the world had never before experienced the scale of combat aircraft manufacture that existed at that time. A few of these aircraft were literally covered with the personal signatures of the factory workers involved in the manufacture of them, and there is some evidence to suggest that some of these grotesquely decorated warplanes actually carried these markings into combat. A minor example of this type of graffiti was carried on the rear of the

Below: 'Nite Train to Memphis', a four-engined C-130 Hercules transport attached to the 164th Tactical Airlift Group which was operational during the 1991 Gulf War against Iraq.

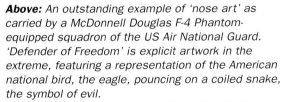

Above: An outstanding example of 'nose art' as carried by a McDonnell Douglas F-4 Phantom-equipped squadron of the US Air National Guard. 'Defender of Freedom' is explicit artwork in the extreme, featuring a representation of the American national bird, the eagle, pouncing on a coiled snake, the symbol of evil.

Above right: 'Big Red 1', an F-106 of the 87th Fighter Interceptor Squadron, in bullish mood.

Above, far right: The RU-21 'Sportsman' featuring bold graffiti and a rather subdued figure which appears to be a surfer.

Right: 'Night Rider', a US Navy C-130 Hercules, is probably named after the successful 1980's TV series featuring a futuristic black-painted car with incredible capabilities.

fuselage on the RAF Coastal Command Lockheed Hudson bomber 'Spirit of Lockheed Vega Employees'.

This type of captioning flourished in Great Britain on combat aircraft produced in both world wars, on what were known as 'Presentation Aircraft'. These aircraft, in line with official instructions, were marked in four-inch yellow letters on the engine cowlings of fighters and under the cockpits of bombers. The names printed on these presentation types were suggested by the sponsor or donors, and were applied to random aircraft leaving the production line and not to individually ordered models as is generally thought. Sometimes the donor's identity was obvious, such as in the case of a Spitfire named 'London Transport', but other donors remain anonymous with names like 'Man of Metal' or 'Sans Tache'. There were no less than four Spitfires named 'City of Birmingham'. Spitfires, as might be expected, were decorated with more of these presentation details than any other Royal Air Force aircraft type during World War II.

Above: 'Spirit of Indiana', a USAF KC-135. The graffiti identifies the home state of the unit.
Left: 'Have Gun Will Travel', an A-10 of the 511th Tactical Fighter Squadron deployed from Alconbury, England, to King Fahd airport in late December 1990 in defence of Saudi Arabia. The artist, J. Trago, was responsible for artwork on many of the unit's aircraft. The artwork features a faceless character in traditional Arab dress leading a camel which packs a large gun on its saddle – possibly a representation of the A-10's fearsome 30mm GAU-8/A seven-barrelled rotary cannon.

At squadron level another variation of official graffiti was that which was applied to combat aircraft to mark a significant anniversary or occasion. This practice seems to have originated at the end of World War II, although some modest examples did occur on Allied aircraft during the course of the war. These rather mundane examples of graffiti were frequently hurriedly painted captions on the noses of selected aircraft that proclaimed such landmarks as '1000 tons of bombs delivered to Berlin' or other inscriptions of a similar nature. Often they were photographed with smiling crew members pointing at them for wartime propaganda use. Similar photos were taken during the Korean War (1950-53). In the ensuing years, peacetime messages such as 'Fly Safe' and '10,000 Accident Free (Flying) Hours' were not uncommon. Squadron anniversaries were occasions that

Above: *Another example of Trago's work on the A-10 'Freedom War-Hog' of the 511th TFS during the Gulf War. Symbolism is rife – the eagle representing the US; the cross, religion; and the aircraft, the awesome power of the USAF.*

Left: *Pieces of official artwork appear on this RAF Hercules – badges of units flying the type – to celebrate the C-130's 25 years of service.*

inspired a modicum of low-key graffiti, but the practice of using these infrequent events to totally repaint an aircraft in garish colours – at least temporarily – has now become widespread, first in NATO and, more recently, in the air forces of Eastern Europe. Even the normally subdued Japanese Self Defense Air Force (JSDAF) has adopted this delightful fashion. An annual NATO event, 'The Tiger Meet', had modest origins but, as the 'International Air Tattoo' held in 1991 at RAF Fairford concurrently with the 'Tiger Meet' was to show, the event has now escalated into a grand contest in which, as a matter of pride, each of the involved 'Tiger' squadrons try to outdo each other with truly spectacular temporary colour schemes which literally dazzle spectators.

US naval graffiti

One category of graffiti is unique to the US Navy and is very rare indeed. The extraordinary practice of completely covering an aircraft with all kinds of derogatory comments, usually painted in removable water-based paint, occurs when an unfortunate naval aviator happens to land his aircraft on the 'wrong' carrier. During operations when several carriers of a task force are stationed in a confined area of latitude and longitude, pilots who have become 'temporarily disorientated', i.e. lost, have been known to touch down on a carrier to which they are not assigned. On such occasions it is a naval tradition

Right: *'The High and Mighty One' carries instantly recognisable 'nose art' of a USAF fighter – an American eagle unleashing a Sidewinder air-to-air missile from its talons.*
Below: *A play on words appearing on the nose of an A-10 displays a degree of modesty not always apparent in artwork. Again, an aircraft of the 511th Tactical Fighter Squadron.*

Above: *RAF 'nose art' on a Tristar tanker, deployed operationally for the first time in the Gulf. The type's nickname, 'Pink Pig' (a term coined from the camouflage applied during the war and its 'tubby' shape), is echoed in the pig-like emblem.*

Left: *The RAF Tornado 'Triffid Airways' shows off its colours during the war to liberate Kuwait. A second motto, 'Watch out for the sting', appears to the left of a representation of one of John Wyndham's more famous creations.*

to send the offending pilot back to his own ship with every type of rude remark adorning his errant aircraft. The remarks often refer to the perceived quality of the offending pilot's airmanship and sometimes the name of his carrier is over-painted with the name of the ship on which he accidentally landed. The worst insult of all, of course, is to have the comment 'Must be Air Force' wryly painted on one's machine. A few years back, Royal Navy Phantoms temporarily based on a US carrier also received this treatment before returning to HMS *Ark Royal*. They received US national insignia and had 'Royal Navy' over-painted with 'Colonial Navy'.

'Zapping'

The last type of common graffiti found on aircraft is not of the written variety but consists of small stencils or stickers that mysteriously appear on warplanes visiting airfields which they do not normally frequent. These markings have come to be known as 'Zaps'. Some of the earliest recorded examples of 'Zaps' were small red-

stencilled kangaroos and kiwis which appeared on RAF and US military aircraft that had taken part in military exercises in Australia or New Zealand. While the origin of this practice is not certain, it would probably be safe to assume that it started 'down under'. Once again, what would appear to be a relatively local and harmless prank proliferated and the practice has now become an almost standard, if unofficial, military procedure.

As with most things, 'Zapping' has become more refined with the passage of time and, occasionally, it does get out of hand. Entire aircraft have been completely repainted overnight while waiting in 'transient parking' spots for overseas aircraft. This sort of excess has led to the practice of posting 24-hour guards, when available, to ensure that the visiting aircraft escapes such treatment. Removing small stickers is not a great problem; however, the removal of a complete unauthorised paint scheme costs time and money. One notorious 'Zap' was an RAF Harrier visiting a base in Germany which ended its visit having been totally covered in pink paint. The unit's commanding officer was not amused. Fortunately this kind of excess is rare and the current 'state of the art' is to surreptitiously apply a small sticky patch, a variation on the

Above: *An RAF Tristar tanker with a more appropriately coloured version of a 'pink pig' (see opposite) and the names of several crew members.*
Right: *Echoes of the George Lucas 'Star Wars' trilogy on the side of an RAF VC 10 tanker of 101 Squadron which is based at RAF Brize Norton in Oxfordshire, England. Each aircraft silhouette indicates one refuelling mission carried out during the 1991 campaign in the Gulf.*

World War II 'Kilroy was here', in a strategic location that would only be uncovered once the aircraft had finally returned to base. The patches themselves vary in subject matter, size and quality, and range from traditional squadron badges to rude slogans. It seems that practically all air arms are now prone to this activity and it is a universally accepted, if not condoned, practice.

Over the years that aircraft have been subject to the application of graffiti, the quality of the 'work' can be said to be of a variable but often high standard. It seems that most military units have been fortunate enough to have a sign painter or amateur artist in their ranks, who has been more than willing to come forward and express his artistic talents. Those that couldn't, probably engaged the talents of local civilian artists to do the job.

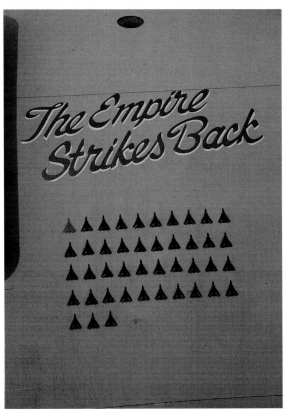

MICKEY AND FRIENDS

The cinema, strip cartoons and, more recently, television have provided a wealth of characters, particularly animals and voluptuous women, that have inspired some of the most outstanding and popular forms of 'nose art'.

Cartoon and comic strip characters, film stars and TV heroes, whether animal or human, have always been popular forms of 'nose art'. Inspiration for these motifs can come from several sources – newspaper or comic strip cartoons and, perhaps more importantly, from the cinema. Cartoon characters, particularly those shown around the world on movie or television screens, frequently transcend national borders; indeed, the same figures can often be found on the aircraft of warring nations. For example, Walt Disney's Mickey Mouse appeared on both Republican and Nationalist aircraft during the Spanish Civil War and proved very popular with the Luftwaffe, among other air arms, in World War II.

Mickey, Bugs and Donald go to war

Why are cartoon and comic strip characters such a widespread phenomenon? First, they are well-known, easily recognisable and colourful. Consequently, reference material for any squadron artist would be easy to find. Second, characters are invariably comical, each having a distinctive personality: Mickey Mouse is the plucky little guy battling against authority; Bugs Bunny is the smart-talking, wisecracking anti-hero; and Donald Duck is the non-too-smart but hard-headed common man.

All of these characteristics are likely to appeal, in one way or another, to fliers who are putting their lives on the line day in and day out, and are a relatively simple way of personalising a particular aircraft in a manner that is unlikely to attract any official censure – unless, of course, the creations are engaged in any risque activities or are coupled with unacceptable language or sayings. However, authorities are generally happy to have the message removed and let the artwork itself remain. The basic images are easily modified to take on a more warlike look, particularly one that reflects the tactical or strategic mission of the particular aircraft. Finally, these representations of famous, much-loved characters are widely recognised as one of the most successful morale-boosters as they are powerful reminders of happier and more carefree pre-war days and a way of life worth returning to once the war is over.

Left: *Jets dogfight over the Yalu River during the Korean War. In this case, 'WHAM BAM', a USAF F-86F Sabre of the 4th Fighter-Interceptor Wing flying out of Kimpo, downs a MiG-15.*

Another general point worth making about cartoon art is that, while some characters stand the test of time, many others tend to be the victims of fashion. Disney's stable of stars have appeared on aircraft from World War II to the Gulf War, yet others, such as the numerous creations that appeared in the 'L'il Abner' strip which achieved great popularity in World War II, have fallen out of favour, to be replaced by characters out of 'Viz', the English comic, or new heroes of either the screen or the comic book. Today, 'nose art' is more likely to consist of Bart Simpson or a Teenage Mutant Ninja Turtle rather than one of the hillbillies taken from artist Al Capp's Dogpatch characters in 'L'il Abner'.

However, in World War II USAAF aircraft in every theatre of operation carried some of Capp's famous creations. For example, several of

Below: No prizes for guessing the wartime role of this RAF Spitfire 'I Spy' – photo-reconnaissance. The heavily stylised dark-blue devil appears to be floating on a small cloud and holds a telescope.

Bottom: An excellent example of World War II cartoon 'nose art' on a US Grumman Wildcat. It features Felix the Cat, in aggressive mood, about to throw a fizzing shell.

the P-47s of the 56th Fighter Group based in England carried Capp-inspired images such as Hairless Joe and the Indian Amaposa; in the Pacific the Mustang-equipped 47th Fighter Squadron, known as the 'Dogpatchers', had many aircraft decorated with similar cartoon characters. Pappy was perhaps one of the most popular of Capp's figures to adorn aircraft noses.

Disney and the 'Flying Tigers'

Though many cartoons inspired 'nose art', it was Walt Disney who did most to popularise the characters that have appeared on aircraft. In fact, Disney, who had been an ambulance driver during World War I, began his long association with war art by painting devices onto trucks attached to his unit and leather jackets. Perhaps his most renowned contribution to the field of aircraft art were the designs he completed for Claire Chennault's American Volunteer Group (AVG), better known as the 'Flying Tigers', which fought the Japanese in the skies over Burma, Indochina and China. The three squadrons of the unit – the 'Hell's Angels', the 'Polar Bears' and the 'Adam and Eves' – were credited with over 300 'kills'. Members of Disney's studio were responsible for the unit's original badge: a winged tiger flying through a 'V' for victory sign. Other designs added to the group's P-40 Tomahawks were sharksmouths – apparently inspired by the RAF's No 112 Squadron which flew ground-attack missions in

Centre left: Artwork on a Boeing Stearman features a baby boy firing a Gatling gun.
Left: A battling bumblebee/ant pictured on the forward fuselage of an RAF Spitfire.
Below: A piece of extravagant 'nose art' on the side of a P-51 Mustang featuring a shower of swastika 'kill' markings – a graphic example of this aircraft's combat effectiveness – and a baby cartoon character holding a heavy machine gun and what appears to be a riding crop. A flash of lightning completes the picture.

Top: A US Navy Hellcat in the livery of Lieutenant Alex Vraciu, who flew the type with Navy Fighting Squadron VF-6.

Above: Walt Disney's most famous creation appears on aircraft of all ages and all nations. This subdued re-creation of Mickey with umbrella was painted on the side of a Luftwaffe Bf 109E-7. The aircraft, flown by Unteroffizier Klick, was shot down over London on 15 September 1940 during the Battle of Britain.

Right: A US Navy Hellcat with excellent artwork of a 'sloppy' wolf.

Above left: One of Walt Disney's most memorable creations for the film 'Snow White and the Seven Dwarfs' appears on 'Grumpy', a B-25 Mitchell.
Above: It was not just the 'big boys' who received a paint job in World War II. This scout carries a portrait of Pappy, one of Al Capp's hillbilly characters who appeared in the extremely popular 'Li'l Abner' comic strip.
Left: The famous B-17 'A Bit o' Lace' with artwork inspired by the siren out of Milt Caniff's much-read World War II comic strip 'Male Call'.

North Africa – and individual squadron emblems based on their names. Unusually, the AVG's winged tiger was requested by an official body, the China Defense Supplies Bureau based in Washington. Interestingly, when the 'Flying Tigers' were disbanded, the insignia, in a slightly modified form, was carried by aircraft of the USAAF's 23rd Fighter Group and, later, the Fourteenth Air Force as a whole.

While his work with Chennault's 'Flying Tigers' is perhaps best remembered, Disney and his team of artists were responsible for

Above: King George VI reviews members of the famous dambusting 617 Squadron lined up in front of Lancaster 'Frederick III'. The cartoon, of a both saintly and angelic individual keeping mum while dropping a bomb, is probably a caricature.

Left: The USAAF's 489th Bombardment Group B-29 Superfortress 'Miss Lace' with artwork inspired by Milt Caniff's creation.

originating many hundreds of insignia for all branches of the US armed forces and many other countries. When World War II ended, the studio had been responsible for the creation of an estimated 1200 pieces of artwork, though not all of them appeared on aircraft. Some, for example, were used on naval vessels, armoured vehicles and leather jackets. Requests for Disney artwork began in the late 1930s when a US Navy officer asked Disney to create a squadron insignia for his unit, VF-7. However, it was the United States' entry into World War II that really spurred the studio on to bigger and better

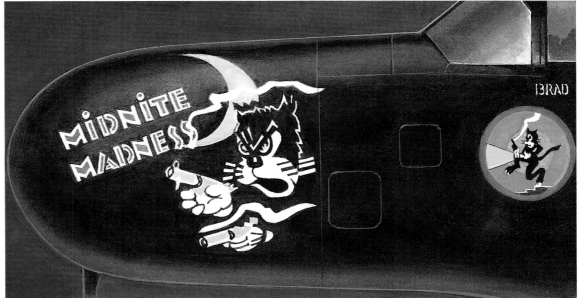

Above: *The Douglas C-47 Dakota was the outstanding transport of World War II. On this example, a fiercely bearded deputy enjoys a cigar.*
Above right: *There's no doubting the prime function of this C-47 with its motto of 'We Deliver', complete with a rough approximation of a stork holding a basket in its feet.*
Right: *'Midnite Madness', a Northrop P-61B Black Widow attached to the USAAF's 7th Air Force's 548th Night Fighter Squadron. Its night-time role is clearly evident in the artwork – smoking six-shooters, a quarter moon and torch-carrying cat.*

things. Aside from the established cast of Disney characters – Mickey Mouse, Pluto, the Seven Dwarfs and friends – he and his colleagues (Disney assigned a five-man team to work on 'nose art' projects) designed many original images, often ones that reflected a unit's name or wartime role. For example, the RAF's Eagle Squadrons had, not surprisingly, an eagle emblem; a nightfighter squadron, an owl.

'Tokyo Bound' with Bugs Bunny
Whether the Disney characters were newly created or taken from establshed movie 'stars', they were invariably given a more menacing

appearance. Luftwaffe ace Adolf Galland's Messerschmitt Bf109s that he flew in the Spanish Civil War and World War II carried a stylised cigar-smoking Mickey Mouse who carried a pistol in one hand and an axe in the

other. One of the Mosquitoes flying with the RCAF's No 409 Squadron carried an artwork of Donald Duck dressed for bed and carrying a burning candle and blunderbuss, an image that clearly reflected the unit's nightfighting role.

Above left: *A startling and startled piece of artwork painted on the side of the aircraft 'Thunder Pussy', though the cat appears to be taking the painful lightning strike somewhat stoically.*

Above: *A well-executed piece of artwork decorates the cowling of this T-28 Trojan. The figure, a patriotic but pugnacious Irishman positioned between three-leaf clovers, probably reflects the pilot's US homeland and the country of his ancestors. Variations on this theme have remained a favourite with American fliers down the decades.*

Left: *A Swedish-built single-engined SAAB J29 fighter on duty with the United Nations in the Congo. Less official identification includes a stenciled insect of unknown origin wearing flying kit and a hefty pair of boxing gloves.*

Above: A perfect position for a piece of rare US Navy 'nose art' on an A-7 Corsair II serving with VA-195 which, when not at sea, was based at Lemoore Air Force Base, California. In general, the navy takes a much stricter line than the other branches of the armed forces with regard to unofficial art. As in Britain, this may have something to do with the US Navy regarding itself as the 'senior service', and the one which sets the standards that the other three services follow.

Right: A smiling but sinister portrait of a horned, red and black devil displayed on the fuselage of a Harvard trainer stationed at Van Nuys, California.

Far right: Shades of the famous film 'King Kong' on this artwork pictured on the side of a US aircraft.

Similarly, other non-Disney creatures were also modified to reflect the role of the aircraft they were painted on. For example, Felix the Cat, complete with torch and six-shooter, was painted onto the fuselage of the USAAF P-61 Black Widow 'Midnite Madness' that flew with the 7th Air Force's 548th Night Fighter Squadron.

Other, more widespread cartoon characters similarly took on a more aggressive note. Bugs Bunny, a rival to Mickey Mouse in the 'nose art' popularity stakes, has been frequently displayed in a warlike state. In the case of a USAF fighter squadron, for example, he is shown as a gunfighter propping up a bar in a saloon with the legend 'Don't Mess with the Kid'. He also frequently appears alongside his most famous phrase, 'What's up, Doc?', or some other saying that might be appropriate to the unit's mission or the particular conflict in question. 'We're Tokyo Bound Doc' which featured Bugs riding a bomb in the company of Porky the Pig sums up the

role of one bomber that took part in the Pacific campaign during World War II. In the European theatre, the B-17 Flying Fortress 'What's Cookin Doc?' featured the ubiquitous rabbit looking a little worse for wear clutching a bottle of XXXX moonshine as he rode to earth perched on the back of a 500lb bomb.

Yosemite Sam

The film studio that created Bugs, Warner Brothers, has a stable of cartoon 'stars' that have been well-represented on aircraft down the years: Elmer Fudd, Daffy Duck, Wile E Coyote from the Roadrunner series, Yosemite Sam and the Tasmanian Devil to name but a few, remain the most popular and instantly recognisable subjects of cartoon 'nose art'. Again, the individuals are frequently modified to reflect an aircraft's primary role. In the case of Yosemite Sam, for example, the P-51 Mustang 'Six-

Left: *An anti-submarine Lynx of the Dutch Navy with a first-rate piece of 'nose art' depicting the Pink Panther cartoon character as a super-sleuth, complete with deerstalker, examining a Soviet submarine through a magnifying glass.*
Below: *Artwork from a second sub-hunting Lynx with Obelix, a character from the Asterix cartoon books, hauling away a Soviet submarine.*

shooter' had Sam spraying lead from a couple of Wild West revolvers, while one USAF KC-135 tanker from the 379th Bombardment Wing, 'Top Off', features the bearded cowboy holding the nozzle of a petrol pump.

Though Walt Disney was a prime-mover in creating individual artwork in times of war, others also made their own contributions, either based on existing characters or ones dreamed up by some artist. Two examples of this occurred in the United States during World War II. At Lockheed's Vega plant close to Disney's Burbank studio in Hollywood, aircraft rolling off the production line started to sprout 'nose art' in the form of an Elmer Fudd-type character who became known as Strato-Sam. Sam was soon joined by a partner known as Kid Vega. Given

Right: 'Harry' the dog enjoys a bottle of lager despite the fact that his unit, the RAF's No 39 Squadron, was being disbanded. The aircraft is a photo-reconnaissance Canberra.
Below right: A 'goofy' winged dinosaur features on the nose of a Beech 18.
Below: 'Nose art' on the US Forestry Commission Flying Boxcar 'Smokey Bear' features the said bear riding a representation of a Consolidated Privateer. Smokey Bear is used by the Commission to warn the general public of the dangers of leaving fires unguarded in woodland.

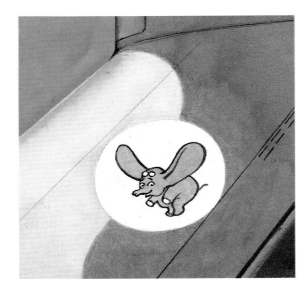

Above: *Walt Disney's Dumbo pictured on the tail of an RAF Tornado of 27 Squadron mimics the unit's official badge which comprises a more traditional elephant on a yellow disc.*
Right: *A slightly battered but unbowed Butch from the 'Tom and Jerry' cartoon series looks out from the side of this US F-15C fighter 'Bulldog One' flown by the unit's commanding officer, Lieutenant-Colonel Thomas Mahan.*
Below right: *Gun-slinging Bugs Bunny props up a bar in this superior example of lovingly created artwork on the aircraft 'Don't Mess with the Kid'.*

the proximity of the Disney headquarters to Lockheed's Vega plant, it was hardly surprising that other aircraft produced at the plant also featured many of his famous creations.

Jane strips for the war effort

While most cartoon characters are usually animal in form, others are much more human and have been used as the inspiration for a wide range of aircraft embellishment. Often the characters in question were voluptuous sirens. In World War II, for example, the strip cartoon character Jane, who appeared in an English newspaper, was a very popular choice for 'nose art', not least because she had a tendency to 'inadvertently' lose her outer clothes in the most innocent situations to reveal frilly underwear. In the United States, a similar effect was created by Milt Caniff's strip cartoons 'Terry and the Pirates' and 'Male Call'. 'Terry and the Pirates' gave aspiring artists around the world such voluptuous and alluring females as Burma, Madame Sho Sho and the mysterious Dragon Lady. All, in one form or another, appeared on every variety of aircraft both during the war and for years afterwards. The story of 'Male Call' is perhaps even more remarkable as the strip, which began in 1942, gave the world the

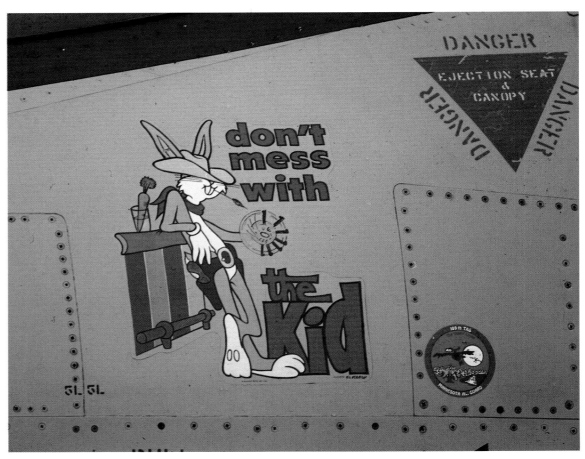

EL COYOTE

Top: Warner Brothers' Wile E Coyote chases after his elusive prey on the side of the Lockheed RP-3A 'El Coyote' of VXN-8.
Above: 'Top Off', depicting a leaping Yosemite Sam offering gasoline, is a USAF KC-135A tanker attached to the 379th Bombardment Wing.
Right: 'Dynamic Duo II', an F-105D Thunderchief of the 192nd Tactical Fighter Group, displays a flying bomb-armed chipmunk and a moose carrying a screwdriver, representing air and ground crews.

Above: *A beautifully executed piece of 'nose art' on a Lockheed RP-3D Orion 'Paisano Tres', again attached to the Maryland-based VXN-8.*

Left: *Another of Warner Brothers' cartoon creations appears on a VXN-8 Orion. This time, the wild and unpredictable Tasmanian Devil adorns the fuselage of the modern reconnaissance aircraft. The unit clearly had an artist who had a gift for painting the cartoon characters created by the studio.*

legendary Miss Lace, who instantly won the hearts of many lowly servicemen as she preferred them, or at least their cartoon equivalents, to officers. She often referred to enlisted men as 'general' or 'admiral', a ploy that couldn't help but endear her to her avid fans.

'A Bit o' Lace'

The most famous aircraft to bear Caniff's artwork was the B-17 'A Bit o' Lace'. Nicholas Fingelly, an artist attached to the USAAF 709th Squadron, 447th Bombardment Group, from late 1943, carried out the work after the Flying Fortress's pilot, John Bauman, presented him

with a detailed sketch of Miss Lace. Bauman had previously written to Caniff asking for permission to utilise the figure and had enclosed a sketch based on the character. Caniff generously responded by returning the outline with an additional message which read, ' "A Bit of Lace" for Lt John H. Bauman and the Gang, with my very best wishes, Milton Caniff, NY, Oct. 1944'. Fingelly got to work and completed the painting in a few hours and gave Milton Caniff full credit for his character. Amazingly, the B-17 survived the war with a tally of over 80 missions. Many squadron artists subsequently made faithful copies of Miss Lace and her colleagues, while others used them as a blueprint for slightly different designs that nevertheless kept to the spirit of the originals. Like the original B-17, the 'Male Call' strip was scrapped shortly after the end of hostilities in 1945. Remarkably, Caniff had been drawing strips for both cartoons throughout much of the war – his was an output unmatched by any other individual artist during the period.

Left: *'Boss Hog', a USAF A-10 that took part in the Gulf War features a mean-looking boar with fearsome tusks carrying a GAU-8/A 30mm cannon. The legend 'Right People, Right Mission, Right Now' also appears on the inside of the access panel.*
Above: *The A-10 'War Pig' carries a similar design to that of 'Boss Hog' but the action takes place at night and the boar holds a bloodied axe.*

Although Caniff's and Capp's creations went out of fashion somewhat after the end of World War II, Disney's creations managed to retain much of their popularity. However, the latter were quickly joined by a multitude of characters taken from the imaginative work of either the Hollywood studios or cartoon artists and, increasingly, from television shows. The Gulf War, for example, clearly demonstrated that although some of the elder statesmen of cartoon 'nose art' retained their popularity, there were many aspiring 'young pretenders' waiting in the wings to usurp their previously paramount positions. Yosemite Sam might still appear on a

Below left: *A friendlier-looking pig listens to some sounds on a portable stereo on the A-10 'Sweet Meat' of the 10th Tactical Fighter Wing. The graffiti reads: 'Dirty Deeds Done Dirt Cheap'.*

Below: *Pigs might fly! A vampirish warthog takes to the night sky in this piece of first-rate 'nose art' that decorates a USAF A-10.*

Above: 'Big Bad Boom', a USAF KC-135 tanker complete with 'Big Bad Wolf' and imperilled pig. Presumably 'boom' refers to the aircraft's inflight refuelling mechanisms.
Right: 'Ridge Runner', a KC-135 of the 79th Bombardment Wing. The hillbilly is based on a Dogpatch character taken from Al Capp's World War II comic strip.

USAF KC-135 tanker but he had to face many newcomers: the suave Pink Panther, to some extent, but more importantly characters from the Bart Simpson TV comic cartoon series and the Ninja Turtles' movies. Elsewhere, aircraft were carrying characters from the 'Garfield' newspaper strip and the remarkably successful British magazine 'Viz'.

Warthogs, war paint and 'Boss Hog'

Other examples of this type of 'nose art' are often not directly based on a specific or slightly modified character but rather reflect some aspect of the particular aircraft or a member of either the air or ground crew turned into a cartoon. For example, a USAF A-10 Warthog was christened 'Fighting Irish' and the 'nose art' consisted of a caricature of a battling Irishman in green, complete with clovers. The image presumably reflects the family origins of one of the pilots and the supposed legendary fighting abilities of the Irish race.

More commonly, A-10s featured creations based on the aircraft's nickname of Warthog. 'Boss Hog', 'War Pig' and 'Playhog' were all names assigned to the Fairchild tank-buster during or just before the Gulf conflict. The first two examples carried menacing caricatures of anthropomorphised wild boars with sizeable teeth and a selection of weapons including the A-10's massive rotary cannon and a bloody axe; the third example had a less warlike pink 'Playboy' Bunny Girl motif. Interestingly, several examples of 'nose art' on the A-10s were hidden away behind access panels, being visible only when the aircraft were being overhauled or prepared for a combat mission. F-117 Stealth fighters also generally carried this type of 'hidden' artwork, though whether this was to mollify higher authority or prevent any reduction in the aircraft's radar 'invisibility' is a matter of conjecture.

Bart Simpson, teenage rebel at war

Many other cartoon characters appeared on aircraft in the Gulf and, given the fact that many of these aircraft, particularly among the RAF squadrons committed to the war, were given a pink desert camouflage scheme, it is hardly surprising that the famous Pink Panther character was to be seen on many aircraft. One example, painted onto the fuselage of a three-engined Tristar long-range inflight refuelling tanker, had the character drawn in stylised formal evening wear, sporting a top hat and leaning on a cane.

Bart Simpson, the most recent cartoon hero to grab a worldwide audience, was much in evidence during the conflict. The bizarrely coloured and youthful rebel with a fine line in pithy, cutting one-liners had obvious appeal to squadron artists. One USAF F-16C Fighting Falcon of the 363rd Tactical Fighter Wing's 17th Squadron had the little guy, who was preparing to unleash a vicious-looking slingshot, saying 'Eat my shorts Hussein'. An A-10 Warthog tank-buster also received the Simpson treatment, showing Bart 'skateboarding' to earth on a Mk 20 Rockeye cluster bomb and shouting his unique war cry of 'Tawakalna Dude'.

....

Above right: A B-52 heavy long-range bomber of the Strategic Air Command's 5th Bombardment Wing, known as the 'Magicians – Best in SAC'. A stylised Arab wizard with enormous turban and outstretched arms completes the art.

Right: Front-on view of the Strategic Air Command B-52 'Ace in the Hole' with mysterious 'Dark Knight' artwork under the pilot's position.

Top: *Flying with the 5th Bombardment Wing out of North Dakota's Minot Air Force Base, the B-52 'Dak Bat' shows off its 'nose art' for the camera.*
Above: *A belligerent Donald Duck prepares to launch a fizzing bomb on an unsuspecting enemy. The artwork appears on the side of the 379th Bombardment Wing's B-52 'Let's Make a Deal'.*
Left: *'Big Smoo II', a B-52 attached to the 2nd Bombardment Wing which flies out of Barksdale Air Force Base, Louisiana. The character appeared in Al Capp's 'L'il Abner' comic strip.*

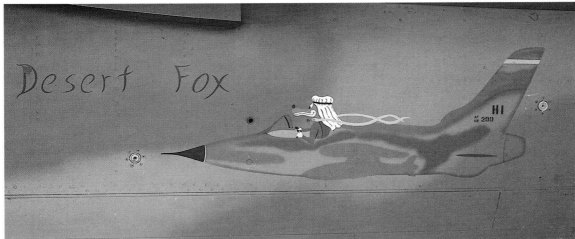

Above: *'Sabre One', an F-16 Fighting Falcon of the USAF, shows off its classic artwork – an armoured, sword-wielding knight complete with flowing cloak and plumes.*
Left: *A turbaned fox pilots an unidentifiable US aircraft; a piece of distinctive fuselage art that appeared underneath the port intake of the fighter 'Desert Fox'.*
Below left: *Bart Simpson, the contemporary cartoon anti-hero, pictures on the nose of the A-10 'Tawakalna Dude...'. Bart rides atop a crude rendition of a Mk 20 Rockeye cluster bomb.*

A host of similarly new cartoon characters made their 'nose art' debut in the same campaign. Chief among the newcomers were a host of creations from one of England's rudest and most successful 'adult' comics – 'Viz'. This magazine provided a wealth of images for the artists: the Fat Slags, Johnny Fartpants and Buster Gonad, to name but a few. The Fat Slags probably won the popularity stakes, appearing on several aircraft including an RAF GR 1 Jaguar and a Hercules transport. In keeping with the 'seaside' feel of the desert, the latter example had the pair dressed in swimming costumes and playing with a beach ball. It seems that higher authority took a dislike to the artwork, in part due to the strict Muslim rules regarding the portrayal of women, and the offending 'nose art' was swiftly removed.

Garfield over the Gulf

The 'Viz' gang were exclusively pictured on RAF aircraft though other characters, like Mickey Mouse before them, appeared on aircraft of many of the Coalition forces. Garfield, the feline hero of the newspaper strip, and his friends were spotted on both USAF and RAF aircraft. The GR 1 Tornado 'Flying High'

Above: The sharp end of the A-10 tank-buster 'Fighting Irish'. This Warthog, normally based at RAF Alconbury with the 511th Tactical Fighter Squadron, was credited with 67 combat sorties in the Gulf. The artwork was completed by D. McCartney.

Above right: 'No Respect', a KC-135A tanker, was obviously involved in some fraught inflight refuelling missions. A heavily laden 'paratrooper' figure has a painful grip on the aircraft's refuelling boom.

Right: The four Teenage Mutant Ninja Turtles proved a popular 'nose art' subject in the Gulf. Here, an A-10 shows off one of the turtles, with the somewhat obscure motto 'Kawabunga'.

featured the cat hitching a lift on a paper plane; a thought bubble appeared above his head but the message, presumably censored by a higher authority, had been erased. One USAF A-10 of the 511th Tactical Fighter Squadron had one of Garfield's chums, the dog Poo, disgustingly

Right: A more menacing image of the dog Butch from the 'Tom and Jerry' cartoon series pictured on the side of a USAF KC-135 strategic tanker.

vomiting up a Hughes Maverick guided air-to-surface missile.

Another comic book/film quartet to make their debut in the Gulf conflict were the Teenage Mutant Ninja Turtles – Donatello, Michelangelo, Raphael and Leonardo – the sewer-dwelling, pizza-loving enemies of evil. These swashbuckling Hollywood creations in green, who have appeared in two box-office smashes, were seen on aircraft as diverse as Boeing KC-135 tankers and Fairchild Republic A-10 Warthogs and often, though not always, were accompanied by their slogan 'Kawabunga' and their vicious-looking Samurai swords.

Left: Many RAF aircraft deployed to the Gulf were soon covered with artwork depicting characters from the 'satirical' English magazine 'Viz'. The artwork appearing on the Jaguar GR 1 'Fat Slags' was one of several pieces completed by Paul Robins before the end of hostilities.

Below left: Another 'Viz' character, the flatulent Johnny Fartpants, appears on a Jaguar based at Muharraq, Bahrain, during the conflict.

Below: Jaguar 'Buster Gonad' – complete with possibly one of the crudest pieces of 'nose art' in the Gulf – photographed for posterity.

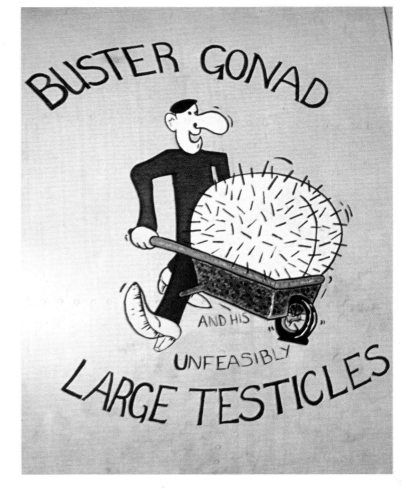

The timeless appeal

As the Gulf War clearly demonstrated, the flier's affection for cartoon characters, from whatever source – cinema, TV, newspaper strip or comic book – and however modified, remains undiminished. Many of today's characters would not be instantly recognisable to World War II airmen, but the spirit that inspired the artists to paint them on the side of modern aircraft would certainly be clearly understandable. Creations such as Mickey Mouse, Bugs Bunny and Donald Duck have clearly stood the test of time, others, such as Milt Caniff's wartime servicemen's sirens, now appear rarely. New characters have taken over in many cases, but it remains to be seen whether they will stand the test of time or not.

Far right: *A top-hatted and cane-carrying Pink Panther strikes a nonchalant pose on the side of a Tristar tanker in the Gulf.*

Right: *The 'Beano' comic's leading cartoon character, Dennis the Menace, complete with pop-gun and motto 'Let me at him', appears on the fuselage of an RAF C-130 Hercules.*

Below right: *Betty Boop was never seen like this! The C-130 Hercules 'Betty Boob' pictured in the war against Iraq. The up-dating or manipulation of existing cartoon characters has always been part and parcel of the work performed by artists.*

Below: *Another favourite cartoon character, in this case Charles M. Schultz's Snoopy, appears riding a laser-guided bomb on the side of the RAF Tornado GR 1 'Snoopy Airways'. Snoopy and colleagues appeared in many forms during the war.*

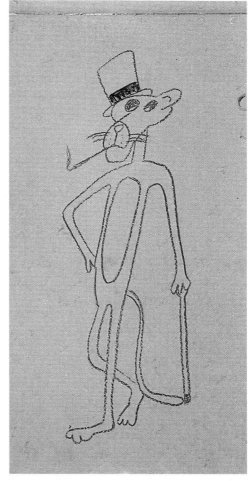

SHARKS AND OTHER ANIMALS

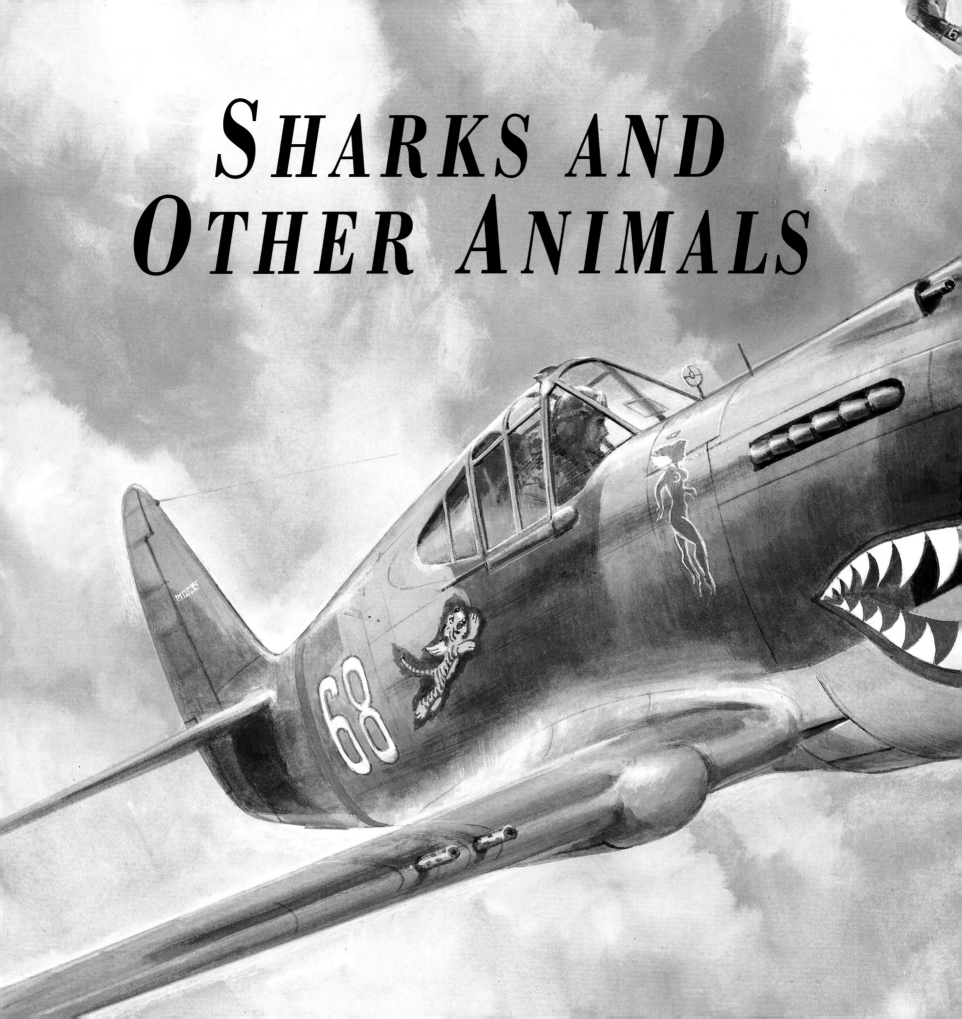

Animals have proved to be an outstanding source of ideas for 'nose art'. Although big cats and sharks are the most widespread and popular examples of the genre, most animals, from the lowly snake to the ponderous elephant, have at one time or another graced aircraft fuselages.

The kingdom of the wild has proved a fruitful and enduring source of raw material for 'nose art' through the ages. Members of the animal world have been so popular for one important reason, a reason that is fairly obvious: wild animals have certain attributes that are often appropriate to their use on aircraft. For example, members of the big cat family, particularly tigers, are among the most fearless and ferocious animals known to man and, though the application of such artwork is especially suitable for fighters, it seems to be regularly applied to every type of aircraft – bombers, transports, helicopters and so forth. One of the USAAF's Flying Fortresses attached to the 388th Bombardment Group's 560th Squadron, 'Tiger Girl', carried an impressive set of jaws which circled the forward gun turret beneath the bomb-aimer's position.

Other animals are also appropriate to certain types of airplane. Elephants, with their ability to carry large loads over great distances, are most suited to long-range transports or inflight refuelling tankers. Some animals, however, are perhaps suitable to all types of aircraft. Rabbits, thanks to their association with good luck – something fliers would like to have in abundance – are a widespread form of 'nose art' and often appear with other good luck symbols – four-leaf clovers, horse shoes and so on.

Sharks and tigers bare their teeth

By no means all of the animals that have been applied to aircraft are of a strong and powerful breed; others are reproduced in a very sorry state, often looking old and decrepit. This often reflects the age, length of service and battle damage suffered by a particular type, and is obviously more likely to be found on aircraft involved in a prolonged conflict such as World War II, Korea or Vietnam, rather than a short-run campaign such as the Gulf War. Examples abound: one such aircraft, the USAF F-86A 'End of the Trail', was transferred after intense combat duty in Korea to the Air National Guard's 146th Fighter Wing at Van Nuys Air Force Base, California, in the mid-1950s. The

Left: A P-40 of Claire Chennault's 'Flying Tigers' in action. This aircraft was attached to the 1st Pursuit Squadron, known as the 'Adam and Eves', and was flown by the ace Charles Older. The winged tiger motif was specially created by Walt Disney.

Top: *A preserved example of a World War I Albatross D Va, one of the Imperial German Air Force's top fighters of 1917. This particular example carries the colours of the machine flown by Leutnant Hans-Joachim von Hippel of Jasta 5 and includes a spectacular piece of 'nose art', a many-legged, fire-breathing red dragon on an already gaudily painted aircraft.*
Above: *An example of one of the best French fighters of the 1914-18 war, the SPAD XIII, features a fine piece of artwork – a swooping eagle with axe picked out in deep red, black and white.*

unit's resident artist applied a paint job that reflected the aircraft's state: a clapped out nag with equally exhausted rider. A second example painted by the same artist, Sergeant Michael Jacobbauski, featured on the F-86 'Un-glued'. The aircraft was so prone to minor glitches that he painted a puny-looking bird of prey plummeting to earth with all of its tail feathers flying off on the forward fuselage.

Despite the fact that many types of animals have adorned the sides of aircraft, two specifically have proved so much more popular subjects than any others – sharks and tigers. Sharksteeth are a true form of 'nose art' in that they invariably appear on the front – nose – of an aircraft rather than the side or elsewhere on the fuselage. Aircraft of all nations have carried such images from World War I to the present day.

'Toothy' designs go to war

In World War II, Luftwaffe Stukas with their huge cowlings and air intakes provided an ideal surface for such work and one unit of Messerschmitt Bf 110 long-range escort fighters, *Zerstörergeschwader* 76, also carried sharksteeth. However, two other units – both Allied fighter-bomber outfits – gained the greatest renown wearing such 'unfriendly' artwork: the Royal Air Force's No 112 Squadron and Claire Chennault's American Volunteer Group, better known as the

'Flying Tigers'. The RAF squadron flew ground-attack missions in the North African and Italian campaigns, while Chennault's Group was active in the Far East, notably Burma and China. Interestingly, both units flew versions of the same aircraft, the Curtiss P-40, and it is alleged that the former's designs inspired the latter's. Whatever the truth of the matter, both units' aircraft were instantly recognisable to friend and foe alike. Certainly, a sharktoothed P-40 diving on the tail of an enemy aircraft or the rear of a fleeing column must have struck fear into the hearts of the enemy's soldiers.

Snarling Phantoms and Corsairs

The phenomenon of sharksteeth was soon taken up by other units in the conflict until every theatre could boast aircraft carrying a toothed design. The example set by both the 'Flying Tigers' and No 112 Squadron of having the whole unit carrying teeth was rare, most other outfits only having the odd one or two aircraft decorated in such a way. This was due to the fact that, unlike Chennault's command, other units did not have their commanding officer's approval

Above, centre: The outstanding Fokker DR 1 triplane that became the favoured aircraft of Germany's top-scoring ace, Baron Manfred, Freiherr von Richthofen. This re-creation of the type has been painted in white and red, and features a bird in flight on the central fuselage.

Above: The cowling of a Wilde Sau (night-fighting) Focke Wulf Fw 190 flown by Oberleutnant Hans Krause of Nachtjagdeschwader 10 during the late summer of 1944 from Werneuchen. Insignia comprises a Wilde Sau (wild boar) emblem with the pilot's nickname 'Illo' picked out in red underneath. Krause gained 28 night victories and was later awarded the famous Knight's Cross.

Left: The Messerschmitt Bf 109 fighter saw service with the Luftwaffe throughout World War II. This preserved example carries an heraldic shield with wolf motif on its forward fuselage.

to undertake such unauthorised non-regulation work. Certainly, it must also be borne in mind that the American Volunteer Group was fighting a long way from home and, perhaps more significantly, its exact position *vis-à-vis* the US armed forces was somewhat ill-defined.

In the years following World War II, sharksteeth or other suitably 'toothy' designs

Left: *The Bell P-63 Kingcobra, with its unusual tricycle landing gear and an engine positioned to the rear of the pilot, proved something of a failure with the USAAF, but over 3000 were sent to Russia under Lend-Lease agreements. This example in Russian colours features a Soviet eagle swooping down on enemy targets – a ship and aircraft. Note the impressive number of 'kills'.*

Below: *A trio of P-40s from the Royal Air Force's 112 Squadron prepare for a sortie over the North African desert during World War II. The teeth were allegedly later copied by the famous 'Flying Tigers'.*

Right: *Modern-day Curtiss P-40s sporting sharksteeth pictured at an air display.*

Above: There's no chance that anyone could mistake this aircraft or the country of its origin. B-17 Flying Fortress 'Mother and Country' features a typical piece of patriotic animal 'nose art' – the US Stars and Stripes and the American bald eagle painted inside a blue and white circle.

continued to appear on many aircraft. The USAF 18th Fighter-Bomber Wing in the Korean War flew Mustangs that had been given sharksteeth under the cowling. However, the design did not, as is usual, feature extremely sharp teeth; rather, they were picked out in a

much more flowing, rounded style in red, white and black. In Vietnam, a conflict which saw wartime 'nose art' make sporadic appearances, at least initially, a wide variety of aircraft sported this fearsome embellishment. McDonnell Douglas F-4 Phantoms, F-105 Thunderchiefs and Vought A-7 Corsairs were perhaps the aircraft most likely to have such works, but many other, less appropriate aircraft also followed the fashion. One electronic countermeasures Boeing EC-130E Hercules attached to the 7th Airborne Command and Control Squadron, which flew out of Korat Air Base in Thailand, was painted

with a set of jaws, albeit until official sanction forced the crew to obliterate their artwork.

Warthogs get mean in the Gulf

In the Gulf War of 1991, many of the RAF's GR 1 Tornado aircraft deployed to the theatre of operations were soon decorated with quite lavish 'nose art'. Aside from the usual pin-ups, cartoon characters, mission markings and so on, many also carried sharksteeth. Usually these would be positioned directly behind the radome, running in a downward curve from just below the pilot's position through the line of the recess housing

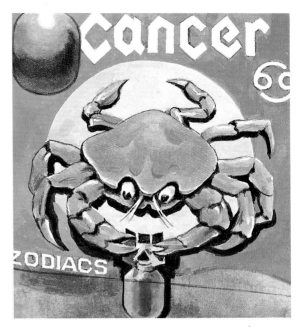

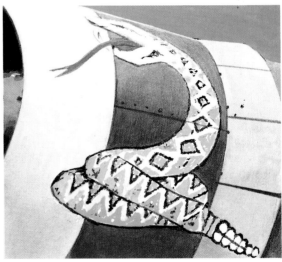

Above left: A broken, 'bag of bones' nag pictured on the side of a presumably clapped out Dakota.

Top: One of a series of outstanding astrological sign artworks produced by renowned World War II artist Philip Brinkman for the B-24 Liberators of the USAAF's 834th Bombardment Squadron. Brinkman completed all of the star signs bar Taurus the bull. In each case the image was finished off with a suitably placed bomb as an obvious comment on the unit's wartime role.

Above: The Korean War also saw some animal artwork. In this case, a coiled rattlesnake seemingly about to pounce has been added to the cowling of an F-4U Corsair of VMF-323. The unit was known as the 'Deathrattlers'.

Left: 'Betty's Dream' (more nightmare, probably) was a B-25J serving with the 345th Bombardment Group (Medium) in the Pacific during World War II. The artwork appears to be a highly stylised dragon.

the 27mm guns, under the fuselage and back out. The colours of the design were not always the standard red, black and white; some were simply red and light blue. In addition, the teeth themselves had a much more curved and flowing look than is normally the case.

Although many fighters of the Coalition forces carried similar designs, the aircraft that carried the most artistically produced and menacing artwork were the USAF's Fairchild Republic A-10 ground-attack aircraft. Warthogs have the ideal nose to take the artwork: slightly squashed, rounded and elongated. The forward-firing rotary cannon bursting out from

Left: *An F-4 Phantom banks to the right during a practice combat mission. In general, 'nose art' was somewhat subdued during the 1960s and 1970s, in part due to the authorities wanting to maintain the effectiveness of camouflage schemes. However, sharksteeth were deemed acceptable.*
Below: *Some F-4 units obviously saw 'nose art' as another form of unit insignia!*

underneath the fuselage and thrusting out between the jaws of any artwork, coupled with large slanting eyes, gave the A-10s in this warpaint a terrifying visage that must have scared many Iraqis out of their wits. Colouring was, for the most part, the standard red, black and white, though some A-10s carried less vivid paint jobs, often in white with black shading (see page 25). Some fighters had teeth in a subdued grey that blended in closely with the standard camouflage coloration, and therefore could not be accused of reducing the aircrafts' 'invisibility'.

Big cats, like sharks, are among the most common and popular type of animal to appear on

Right: French-built Dassault Mystére IVAs on display in a museum. The central aircraft carries what appears to be a flying swan in black and white on the forward part of the fuselage.

Below right: A Huey transport helicopter in action during the Vietnam War with a prancing, fire-breathing dragon displayed across the nose. The creature carries both a trident and shield.

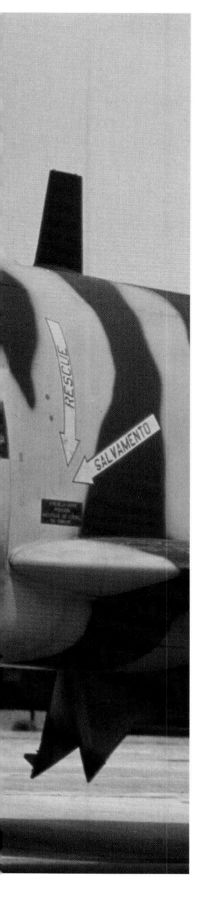

Above: *The unmistakable tailplane of an F-18. This example, currently flying with the Canadian Air Force, features a restrained rendition of a tiger.*

aircraft, either as traditional 'nose art' which might feature a small example of a whole creature or a large artwork of its head, or, more unusually, as a specifically designed paint scheme covering the majority or even the whole of the aircraft that has been permitted by higher authority for some airshow or commemorative event. In World War II, Walt Disney was commissioned to create a suitable unit emblem for Claire Chennault's American Volunteer Group. He came up with a symbol that gave the Group its more widely remembered name – the 'Flying Tigers' – and his work was painted on the fuselages of the unit's P-40s, usually slightly to the rear of the cockpit and trailing edge of the wing. The design also surfaced on badges and commemorative tie-pins. Similar motifs also appeared on the aircraft of other combatants in the war. For example, leading Luftwaffe ace Major Heinz Barr flew a Messerschmitt Bf 109 that had a pouncing lion leaping from an heraldic shield positioned just forward of the cockpit.

The most superb modern-day examples of aircraft carrying tiger 'nose art' are to be found at

Far left: *An outstanding illustration of the high quality of artwork that appears at NATO-sponsored 'Tiger Meets'. This stunning example is a Fiat G-91R belonging to the Portuguese Air Force's 301 Squadron pictured at RAF Fairford, July 1991. Such officially sanctioned schemes are removed when the aircraft return to their parent units.*

Top left: *Camouflage more appropriate to the jungles of India has been painted on this tigerish CF-104 Starfighter from Canada.*

Above left: *The French Air Force was one of the creators of the 'Tiger Meet'. Here, a home-grown Mirage F1 reveals its new colours.*

Left: *An American-designed fighter – the F-16 – in the colours of a Belgian tiger squadron.*

Above: The Royal Air Force also has a few units that are entitled to enter the 'Tiger Meet' competitions because their official badge includes a tiger, though not all fly fighters. This lavish piece of art appears on a relatively humble SA 330 Puma transport helicopter belonging to 230 Squadron.

the International Air Tattoo 'Tiger' Meets, a NATO-sponsored meeting that began in 1961 which brings together aircraft of all types from squadrons that have a big cat in their official unit emblem. Since its inception, when aircraft from just three countries – France, the United States

and United Kingdom – took part, the event has grown in popularity to such an extent that more than a dozen countries attended the 30th Anniversary 'Tiger Meet' which was held at RAF Fairford in 1991. Aircraft and units present included the Royal Canadian Air Force's 439

Squadron which flies CF-18A/Bs, Turkey's 192 Squadron which flies F-104 Starfighters out of Balikesir, and Portugal's Fiat G-91-equipped 301 Squadron. The Fairford event also marked a departure from tradition: perhaps reflecting the radical changes in Eastern Europe, MiG-29

Fulcrums of the Czechoslovakian Air Force's 11 (Tiger) Regiment were on display. The unit had been made an honorary member of the Tiger Association for the show.

The aircraft present at the meetings are covered with what can only be described as

Above: When tigers meet! Two Royal Netherlands Air Force F-16 Fighting Falcons – part of the country's total of 180 – at an International Air Tattoo, complete with tailplanes covered in first-rate 'nose art' of a pair of roaring tigers, await the arrival of the judges' decision.

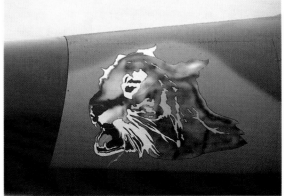

Top: *The 'Tiger Meets' have gradually expanded since the first was held in 1961. Nowadays, jets from even the most far-flung NATO members attend, as in the case of this F-104 Starfighter from Turkey's 192 Squadron based at Balikesir.*

Above centre: *A tiger's head as painted onto the side of an RAF Tornado of an unidentified unit.*

Above: *An F-111 of the USAF's 20th Tactical Fighter Wing parked at Fairford. This particular F-111 saw service in the Gulf where it made 22 sorties piloted by the 79th Tactical Fighter Squadron's commanding officer.*

Left: *A painted Royal Navy S-61 Sea King HAS.5 maritime helicopter of 814 Squadron based at Culdrose, Scotland, in attendance at the 1991 'Tiger Meet' at RAF Fairford.*

officially sanctioned 'nose art'. The onus is on the 'home' unit or units to provide the most dazzling and original work, though competition for the silver tiger award, presented for the 'best of show', is strong. The paint jobs vary in colour, style and extent. Some aircraft at a recent meeting were decorated in orange and black, others in yellow and black, while one Canadian unit provided a CF-18 that had been given a camouflaged two-tone grey tiger skin. Countries taking a more traditional view of the competition painted either simple tiger stripes or went the whole way with elaborate heads complete with fearsome teeth. Either way, the 'nose art' on display is temporary and removed when the particular aircraft returns to its parent squadron.

The concept of boosting morale and creating a cohesive force through the use of such themes

Right: *An F-15 Eagle carries its namesake picked out in white, yellow and black. The use of animal 'nose art' to identify the official name of an aircraft is fairly common; equally, unofficial names, usually of a derogatory nature, are also commemorated with appropriate art.*

Below right: *'Ole Baldy II', a B-52 Stratofortress of the USAF's Strategic Air Command that saw action against Iraq in 1991. The 'nose art' of an eagle with a bomb in its talons is a faithful copy of a motif appearing on a World War II B-24.*

Below: *The Vought A-7D Corsair 'War Eagle' of the South Carolina Air National Guard on temporary deployment to RAF Wittering shows off its colours – an eagle, obviously in flight, holding a bomb against a 'V' for victory sign. Air National Guard units often tend to have a more relaxed attitude to what constitutes acceptable artwork.*

Above left: A rare piece of 'nose art' behind the air intake of a Czech Air Force L-39 Albatross. The rather geriatric albatross insignia probably reflects the aircraft's name and age.

Top: Birds of prey, because of their ferocity and superb flying skills, have always appealed to artists. This fine example appears on the side of a USAF B-52 flying with the 28th Bombardment Wing.

Above: Occasionally 'nose art' reflects the theatre of operations of an aircraft. This penguin has been painted onto a Royal Navy Wasp helicopter operating from the ice patrol vessel Endurance.

Left: A crude example of artwork applied on exercise appearing on the side of Australian Chinook 'The Wallaby Express'.

Top: *The Royal Air Force rather frowns on 'nose art', both in peace and war. However, occasional aircraft do get the treatment. This F-4 Phantom served with 41 Squadron at RAF Coltishall.*
Above: *A new generation of aircraft have also been fited with teeth. Here, a USAF General Dynamics F-16C of the 52nd Tactical Fighter Wing taxies onto the runway before a sortie.*
Right: *A superb portrait of a USAF McDonnell Douglas F-4 Phantom engaged in a vertical climb during the Team Spirit exercise held at Osan Air Force Base in 1988. Note the classic sharksteeth.*

also surfaced in the work of an artist who served with the USAAF's 486th Bombardment Group that flew out of bases in England during World War II. Philip Brinkman, officially a draughtsman in operations, exercised his art on a series of B-24 Liberators of the Group's 834th Bombardment Squadron after the unit had settled in at Sudbury in Suffolk during April 1944. His paintings, which earned the unit its nickname of the 'Zodiacs', consisted of astrological star signs. All were completed, bar Taurus the bull, and animals abounded: Aries the ram, Cancer the crab, Leo the lion, Scorpio the scorpion and so on. All of the artworks also carried the symbols and names of the signs, and most were finished off with the animals and other images carrying bombs as a means of identifying the wartime role of the aircraft.

Enter the 'Deathrattlers'

Wolves and foxes, either complete or just the head, have appeared on aircraft since World War I. In that conflict, for example, Leutnant Otto Fuchs ('fuchs' translates as fox) of Jasta 77b flew an Albatross D Va which featured a fox chasing a cock (a creature closely associated with the French) along its fuselage. In the next war, wolves appeared on both fighters and bombers.

Below: *A Douglas A3D Skywarrior prepares to take off on a mission. This two-seater US Navy jet was originally designed as a strategic bomber but several were updated for the long-range maritime reconnaissance role, hence the inflight refuelling probe on this 'toothy' model.*

Usually, they were portraits slavering with fangs bared or howling at the moon.

Of the other members of the animal kingdom that appear as 'nose art', reptiles, either real or imaginary, remain a popular subject. With their swift striking movements, fangs and venom,

snakes are most appropriately applied to fighter squadrons. One US Navy unit flying F-4U-4 Corsairs in Korea, VMF-323, was known as the 'Deathrattlers' and some planes carried artwork depicting a coiled rattlesnake raising its head with forked-tongue extended and fangs bared,

ready to strike at its prey. On occasion, snakes lose something of their menace when they are represented in a more cartoon-like manner. One McDonnell Douglas F-4 Phantom flying with an Air National Guard unit had a vividly drawn green and orange snake which looked rather

Below: *A fine view of a Royal Air Force English Electric Lightning of 5 Squadron, featuring the unit's official green maple leaf badge and a fine pair of wickedly smiling jaws, all topped off by a pair of piercing eyes. The unit was the last to fly the venerable Lightning in the UK.*

Bottom: *Sharksteeth on a two-seater English Electric bomber. A few Canberras are still in service with the Royal Air Force undertaking photo-reconnaisance operations, being fitted with a suite of cameras and more powerful engines. The aircraft was the RAF's first post-war jet bomber.*

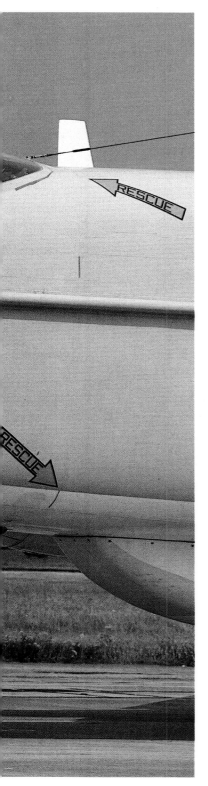

more endearing than warlike, being kitted out with a flying helmet and the motto 'Trussst Me!'. Similarly, dragons are favoured by many artists because they have all the attributes of the aforementioned snakes with the added bonus that they also breath fire. German World War I pilot Leutnant Hans-Joachim von Hippel of Jasta 5 flew an Albatross D V which carried extensive 'nose art' along its fuselage. This consisted of a many-legged green winged dragon that poured fire from its open mouth.

In World War II, one USAAF unit attached to the 38th Bombardment Group, the 405th Bombardment Squadron, earned the nickname of the 'Green Dragons' because the unit's B-25s

Top: *A piece of artwork possibly inspired by Steven Spielberg's highly successful 1970's movie 'Jaws' appears on the KC-10A tanker 'Great White' of the USAF's 68th Air Refueling Wing.*

Right: *The sleek lines of Rockwell's B-1 long-range intercontinental strategic bomber are evident from this picture of 'Wolf Hound' which flies with the 319th Bombardment Wing.*

had been given 'nose art' that consisted of dragons. The design proved so popular that when the squadron switched its North American Mitchell bombers for Douglas A-26 Invaders in the latter stages of the conflict, similar 'nose art' was applied to the new aircraft.

Examples of this type of artwork can still be found up to the present day. During the Gulf War, one B-52 Stratofortress of the 42nd Bombardment Wing, 'First Strike', received the attention of artist H. Paige who completed an outstanding piece of 'nose art'. Paige's creation comprised a green fire-breathing dragon whose body gradually mutated into the fuselage and wings of a B-52. The hybrid was swooping down, with bombs dropping, on its target – a camel representing the regime of Saddam Hussein.

Many other animals have also appeared on aircraft down the decades. Elephants have been seen on C-47 Dakotas and B-29 Superfortress bombers because their essential characteristics of strength and load-carrying capabilities are reflected in the particular aircraft. On occasion,

Left: *A snorting rhino is the centrepiece of the badge of the USAF's 89th Tactical Fighter Squadron, an element of the 906th Tactical Fighter Group of the US Air Force Reserve.*
Below: *A piece of official commemorative 'nose art' has been painted onto the tailfin of this Royal Air Force Tornado F3 to celebrate 65 Squadron's 75th anniversary. The squadron, of Strike Command, is currently based at RAF Coningsby.*
Below left: *'Arkansas Razorback', a B-52G of the 97th Bombardment Wing, shows off its fine tailplane artwork of a wild boar at speed.*

the artwork does not reflect a role but rather the location of an aircraft's base. One helicopter attached to the Royal Navy's patrol vessel HMS *Endurance* which is stationed in the South Atlantic carried a penguin; a USAF KC-135 tanker of the Air National Guard's 168th Air Refueling Squadron, 'Arctic Traveler', featured a polar bear as the unit's base is in Alaska.

When it comes to the animal kingdom as a source of inspiration for 'nose art', it is clear that virtually all of its members, with the exception of the rarely used aquatic world (sharks excepted), have appeared in one form or another. Attributes of the animals are applied to

Above: *A fine example of animal 'nose art' appears on 'Equipoise II', a USAF B-52 Stratofortress bomber attached to the 2nd Bombardment Wing which flies out of Barksdale Air Force Base, Louisiana. The winged horse is presumably a representation of the mythical Pegasus, a creature created from the blood of Medusa.*
Left: *The menace of the A-10 Thunderbolt is evident from this front-on view of an aircraft from the 509th Tactical Fighter Squadron. The artwork is typically patriotic – an eagle holding a machine gun in its talons against a backdrop of a light blue circle.*

individual aircraft, highlighting either their outstanding capability or a particular weakness. Usually, the animals painted on to aircraft are faithful representations of the real thing, often carrying an item or fulfilling a role that is appropriate to the aircraft. National animal symbols or animals associated with a particular country, such as the US eagle or the Canadian moose, also provide a form of identification.

However, animals are occasionally caricatured to identify a particular conflict. In World War II, some animals were given the faces of enemy leaders – Hitler and Mussolini, for example. In the Gulf, animals appropriate to the region, notably camels, appeared as both traditional 'nose art' and as smaller mission/'kill' markings.

Animals then are likely to remain a favourite form of 'nose art', one that unlike many other types is less likely to be a victim of fads and fashions. Cartoon characters, pin-ups and heroes and villains wax and wane in popularity, but sharks, tigers and a whole host of other animals seem set to remain a major source of inspiration for squadron artists in the future.

Above: 'Nose art' on the front of a McDonnell Douglas/BAe AV-8B Harrier onboard a vessel of the US Navy. Subdued artwork of this type seems to be more acceptable to those in authority.
Left: A stork delivers a much more menacing load than is usual in a vivid, well-executed example of Gulf War 'nose art' on the forward fuselage of a USAF B-52 bomber of the 416th Bombardment Wing which is stationed at Griffiss Air Force Base, New York. The 'Special Delivery' line dates back to World War II when it appeared on several bombers including a B-17, a B-25 and a B-29.

PIN-UPS

Of all the images seen as aircraft 'nose art', it is women who have been the most popular subject. Scantily clad sirens, often based on the work of magazine artists, popular film stars and wartime heroines, have all inspired some of the finest – and most controversial – pieces of artwork.

It is hardly surprising that women have proved the most popular and widespread form of 'nose art'. Though such images were generally absent from the aircraft in World War I, probably due to a more puritanical outlook on life, subsequent wars saw an explosion of the art that some found – and find – erotic and others exploitative. Whatever the morality of portraying semi-clad women on aircraft, the reasons for the phenomenon are really not very hard to discern.

War separates youthful men from their wives, sweethearts and mothers and propels them into a predominantly male environment. The situation is essentially unnatural, thus many artworks were undoubtedly created to remind aircrews of a particular woman or womankind in general. The image, therefore, is both sexual and sentimental. Betty Grable, the famous American actress who appeared in many films during the 1930s and 1940s, was the most popular pin-up of World War II. Her legs were allegedly insured for a staggering one million dollars! Grable appeared on many aircraft in the conflict, often in a 'back-to-camera' swimsuit pose that showed off her valuable assets to the full. The image contained a measure of wishful thinking – that the lucky crew might actually meet the celluloid siren – and was also a clear reminder of a common event outside of wartime: going to the cinema. Whatever the case, the image was undoubtedly an idealised portrait of what the men of the time considered the perfect woman.

Clandestine pin-ups in the Gulf

War also breeds a morality entirely different to that which exists in peacetime. Men fighting for their lives many miles from home, with little or no contact with the opposite sex, seem more able to portray women in a base way, i.e. naked or semi-naked and 'available'. While the war continues and there is little chance of their art being seen by the general public, little concern is expressed. However, the end of conflict often changes this situation radically. Many aircraft have returned from hostilities with their risque artwork obliterated with a judicious coat of paint,

Left: A sight to strike fear into the hearts of any ground forces – an A-10 Warthog tank-buster on the attack. This particular aircraft, 'Iron Maiden', flies with the Maryland Air National Guard's 175th Tactical Fighter Group.

Above: *Female 'nose art' on a Lockheed P-38 comprising a leggy, reclining blonde and a piece of graffiti, 'Miss Behavin', that has proved popular down the ages. By playing on words, artists could possibly avoid official censure.*
Left: *'Nose art' on the fuselage of a USAAF Republic P-47 Thunderbolt 'somewhere in England'. 'In the Mood', named after a popular Glen Miller tune, was flown by Robert Johnson, a pilot with the 56th Fighter Group in World War II.*

or the woman, previously nude, in suddenly acquired clothing. This holds good for World War II and, perhaps more surprisingly, the same phenomenon was not unknown during the recent Gulf War. Despite the general strictness of the Saudi Arabian regime with regard to the portrayal of women, many Allied aircraft featured pin-ups. Some were very explicit, yet managed to escape official censure while the war lasted. However, when the aircraft returned to their home bases, there had been a 'cover-up'. 'Foxy Lady', a Royal Air Force C-130 Hercules

Top: The Junkers Ju 52 was the leading German transport of World War II. Here, 'Iron Annie' shows off her martial prowess.

Above: A fine piece of art decorates the forward fuselage of a Douglas A-26 Invader attack bomber. The figure, 'Dream Girl', is obviously the stuff of male fantasies: blonde and long-legged, and about to reveal every inch of her body.

Above right: The tailplane of a preserved of a Royal Air Force P-40 with a standard piece of female art – busty blonde – and a motto that could relate to air or sexual 'combat'.

Right: 'Spirit of Waco', a Douglas A-26 Invader, turns over its engines before a flight. A female, complete with imaginative halo, adorns the aircraft's elongated nose.

involved in special forces' operations, was adorned with an explicit nude figure but, when it returned to RAF Lyneham after the war, the sprawling figure was wearing a bright red bikini.

Another reason for the widespread use of female imagery has much in common with the

Above left: *One of the most famous pieces of World War II 'nose art' appeared on the 91st Bombardment Group B-17 'Memphis Belle'. The artwork was based on a pin-up produced by artist George Petty for* Esquire *magazine. Here, the crew of the 'Belle' attend a parade in England before returning to the US after completing 25 missions.*
Above: *The 'Memphis Belle' appeared in a film by William Wyler in World War II and, more recently, the story of the crew and their last mission was turned into a popular movie. The aircraft above appeared in this 1991 tribute.*
Left: *'Pist'l Packin' Mama', named after a popular song, displays a typical example of pin-up 'nose art', complete with strategically placed gun belt.*
Above right: *'Shoo Shoo Shoo Baby' served with the USAAF's 303rd Bombardment Group and managed to survive the war.*
Right: *'Sentimental Journey' (named after a hit song from World War II) with star Betty Grable.*
Far right: *A blonde caught by surprise while leaving the shower appears on B-17 ' "Lassie, I'm Home" '.*

personalisation of ships and the frequent use of female figureheads: men seem to find it important to endow their charge with a female personality.

Fond reminders of home

As a further reminder of home, the women might appear in some form of national or highly stylised local dress, or would be accompanied by some statement identifying the home of a crew member. Women portrayed as the Statue of

Above: The silver fuselage of a B-17 provides the ideal backdrop for a reclining nude. Such explicit artwork was generally rare in World War II and, in cases where it did occur, it was often censored before the aircraft returned home.

Above right: A fine inflight shot of the preserved B-17 'Sally B' with its bomb-bay doors open. The sprawling female is captured in a typical pose.

Right: 'Target for Tonight' was a B-17 Flying Fortress. The image created by the artist does not refer to the operational cliché but, rather, to the three key elements that could help any airmen to relax – wine, women and song.

Liberty or Britannia would obviously represent the United States or Great Britain respectively, while a pin-up dressed as a cowgirl would more than likely represent Texas. 'Texas Gal', a USAAF B-25 from World War II, featured such a woman dressed in stetson and cowboy boots painted with the lone star of the Lone Star State. In some cases, however, the women might be used to identify a particular theatre of operations. One B-24 attached to the Eighth Air Force and deployed on anti-submarine patrols in the Bay of Biscay off the coast of France

featured a swimsuited type sitting on a bomb; its name was 'Biscay Belle'. In the Gulf War, one Royal Air Force maritime patrol Nimrod MR.2P featured a seven-foot buxom blond named 'Muscat Belle'. The Nimrod was stationed at Seeb in Oman, just a few miles from Muscat itself. Several Tornado GR 1s were named 'Hello

Above left and right: *The source of much inspiration for wartime artists were the famous Esquire magazine gatefolds created by men such as Alberto Vargas. These centrefold calendars also adorned barracks and were used to record the dates and major events of particular raids, as in the case of the two examples shown.*

Top: *Many aircraft in World War II carried pin-ups based, however loosely, on stars from the world of entertainment, particularly film and music. This B-17 features a suitably covered up vision of the famous dancer and partner to the debonaire Fred Astaire, Ginger Rogers. The background consists of a heavily stylised blue cloud.*

Kuwait, G'Bye Iraq' and each featured a nude or semi-nude female artwork. Apart from the usual well-proportioned figures, one example, known as 'Grannie', carried an older woman complete with walking frame!

Probably the most famous aircraft of World War II and the star of a William Wyler documentary made in 1943 and a 1980's film, 'Memphis Belle', combined a name and image that reflected both home and heart. This Eighth Air Force B-17 was the first to complete 25 missions over Europe, during which time its

Right: *Women pictured on aircraft are often dressed in some caricature of national or regional costume. The B-24 Liberator 'Shoot You're Covered' is decorated with a scantily clad cowgirl.*
Below: *A fine view of the North American B-25 Mitchell bomber 'Executive Sweet' with naked – but coyly posed – brunette. Flowing hair and a billowing scarf complete the look.*

crew shot down eight enemy fighters, claimed five probables and 12 damaged. On the crew and bomber's return to the US, they were involved in fund-raising flights and ceremonies across the States. The 'Belle's' unit, the 91st Bombardment Group, arrived in England in late 1942 and was stationed at Bassingbourne, where artist Anthony Starcer provided the skill to complete the artwork. His effort consisted of two long-legged,

Left: *A re-creation of artwork that appeared in a slightly more revealing form on a World War II photo-reconnaisance B-24. The original inspiration came from the February 1945 gatefold created by Alberto Vargas for Esquire magazine.*
Below left: *The drab camouflage of this B-25 'Marvellous Miriam' is enlivened by its 'nose art'.*

Top: *The work of Alberto Vargas was copied by many squadron artists. This particular example was taken from the Esquire gatefold of April 1943 and appears on 'Night Mission', a B-24 that flew in the Pacific with the 30th Bombardment Group.*
Above: *The same Vargas gatefold, but this time on the 308th Group's B-24 'Sack Time'.*

Top left : An unusual example of camouflage can be seen on the heavily modified Consolidated Vultee B-24 Liberator 'Diamond Lil' which also features a fur-draped siren drenched in a 'girl's best friend'. The aircraft was damaged on its way to England and, after conversion to a C-87 cargo-carrier, flew all over the United States.

Top right: The Consolidated B-24 Liberator bomber 'Delectable Doris' shows off its wartime colours including a provocative woman.

Left: 'Mors Ab Alto', which translates as 'Death from Above', was a B-24 that served with the 7th Bombardment Group in the Philippines during World War II. The motif – an avenging angel – is swooping down onto a target. Note also the bomb falling through the clouds to the rear of the heraldic shield.

Above: 'Home Stretch', featuring a blonde struggling to remove her underwear, appeared on a 7th Bombardment Group Liberator. The Group was part of the USAAF's 10th Air Force.

swimsuited pin-ups, one positioned on either side of the nose. On the left-hand side the figure appeared in a blue swimsuit; on the right it was red. Starcer also added mission markings (bomb stencils) and 'kill' symbols (swastikas). The mission markings were further refined with secondary symbols that denoted the aircraft's role in a particular sortie: a yellow star above a bomb indicated the B-17 was the Group's lead ship; a red star, that it was leading a wing. A

variety of names – 'Virginia', 'Irene' and 'Mom', for example – also appeared on the fuselage next to the positions of the crewmen.

Creating the 'Memphis Belle'

The background to the creation of the 'Memphis Belle' artwork provides an interesting insight into the genesis of an item of 'nose art'. The pilot of the aircraft, Bob Morgan, originally intended to call it 'Little One', after his pet

Above: An example of female 'nose art' decorating the fuselage of a US Navy S-3B Viking from the USS America *features the classic combination of a blonde giving a 'come hither' look while perched on what looks like a homing torpedo.*

name for his fiancee, Margaret Polk. However, fate intervened when the crew caught a film starring John Wayne and Joan Blondell called 'Lady for a Night'. Blondell's character was

Below: *F-4G 'G-Wiz Lucille' features a leggy red-head with an immodestly short dress leaning against a AGM-88A HARM missile.*
Below centre: *'The Bad Bitch', an EA-3B, displays erotic artwork clearly based on the popular genre of sword and sorcery literature.*
Below right: *The artwork on this US Navy F-4 of VFMA-321 has much in common with the emblem worn by the Flying Tigers' 1st Pursuit Squadron.*

nicknamed 'Memphis Belle' and, as the crew clearly enjoyed the film and Morgan had close links with the state capital, the name 'Little One' was replaced by 'Memphis Belle'.

Although the name was decided upon, there remained one outstanding problem: where to find an appropriate image? Morgan took as his inspiration the US magazine *Esquire* which was famous for its 'tasteful' renditions of the fulsome

female form. He wrote to the magazine asking for help, and later received a copy of the magazine's April 1941 edition. That issue's centrefold, created by the famous George Petty, provided the guide for Stracer's final work.

The key to the form of the 'nose art' for 'Memphis Belle' was *Esquire* magazine. It was a story that was to have parallels around the globe as aircrews and artists drew inspiration from the

work of a handful of magazine artists, in many cases making a fair copy of the original artwork. Three individuals in particular stand out as contributing most to the field: George Petty, Gillette Elvgren and, most famously, Alberto Vargas. The women portrayed by the three were never completely nude and, indeed, by today's standards would probably be seen as rather tame. Nevertheless, their idealised visions of American womanhood undoubtedly fired the imagination of military airmen around the world. The alluring images produced by all three men appeared in a variety of publications – *Esquire*, advertisements and calendars, for example – that were widely seen both in the United States and overseas, making them a readily available source of inspiration for the wartime artists. Many of the calendar girls also ended up on the walls of airfield buildings, often with specific comments concerning particular sorties made against the relevant dates.

Below: A fine profile of this USAF KC-135 shows off a classic example of female 'nose art'. The witch-like figure with spreading wings is dressed in flowing black robes. The sandy-pink background might be an outline of the aircraft's home state.

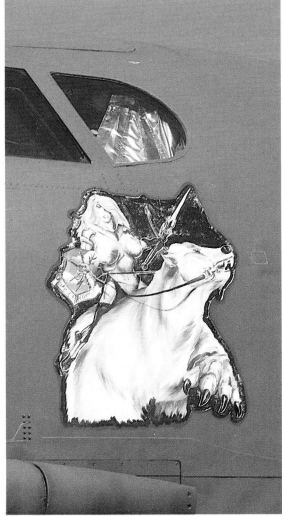

Above: *A fairly battered artwork depicting a sword-wielding 'ice maiden' adorns the side of a B-52H attached to the USAF's 7th Bombardment Wing.*
Left: *A case of 'nose art' echoing down the ages. This KC-135 'Sweet Sixteen' of the 135th Air Refueling Group has artwork based on the Vargas gatefold which saw the light of day in the July 1943 issue of* Esquire *magazine, and appeared on many World War II aircraft.*

The work of Vargas, Petty and Elvgren appeared on all types of aircraft, and are found right up to the present. One of Vargas's creations which was the Christmas 1943 gatefold in *Esquire* illustrates the impact of his work. Among other aircraft, the artwork, entitled in the magazine as 'There'll Always Be A Christmas', which consisted of a flying woman wearing a one-piece swimming costume with a long flowing scarf, appeared on the B-25 'Heavenly Body' in World War II. It has also re-surfaced on a pair of USAF B-52s: 'Special Delivery' of the 92nd Bombardment Wing and 'Diamond Girl' of

Above: *'Net Results', an F-111B which flew out of Plattsburgh Air Force Base, New York, with the 380th Bombardment Wing, consists of a tennis-playing lovely caught up in the net.*
Left: *A common form of modern 'nose art' can be seen on this B-52 of the USAF's 96th Bombardment Wing which is based at Dyess, Texas. 'Polarized' consists of a young woman armed with a sword and shield riding on a muscular polar bear.*

the 410th Bombardment Wing. The artists who worked on these Stratofortresses have added their own touches to the aircraft. The woman on 'Special Delivery' carries a bomb in her right hand, while on 'Diamond Girl' the figure holds a glittering example of 'a girl's best friend'.

Artists have always drawn on published work for their female artworks and, although the women of World War II still make the occasional appearance, they have been superseded by more current and generally more explicit images taken from modern 'girlie' magazines, films and heavy metal/sword and sorcery-type cartoon books. In

the Gulf War, for example, one B-52 called 'Iron Maiden' (the name of a heavy rock band) featured a buxom female warrior armed with sword and shield riding a polar bear, while an A-10 tank-buster of the Maryland Air National Guard, also named 'Iron Maiden', went the whole 'hog' and simply displayed a 'tastefully' arranged naked brunette.

The portrayal of the naked or semi-naked female form is increasingly associated with overtly phallic images and fetishistic apparel. Many A-10s in the Gulf carried such material. Two examples should suffice; 'Panther Princess'

Left: *A mythical reference appears on the side of this USAF 96th Bombardment Wing Rockwell B-1 long-range bomber 'Excalibur'. The sword was carried by King Arthur in battle until it was returned to the mysterious 'Lady of the Lake'.*
Below: *B-52G 'Special Kay' of the 379th Bombardment Wing with a standard piece of explicit nude 'nose art' and an unusual set of mission markings which include an axe or tomahawk, a steam train and a simple sailing vessel.*

of the 353rd Tactical Fighter Squadron featured a bikini and chap-covered blonde sitting astride a GAU-8/A rotary cannon that was spitting fire; 'View to a Kill'(which also happens to be the name of a James Bond film) showed a woman lying along the length of an AGM-65 Maverick guided air-to-surface missile.

The Royal Air Force also got in on the act during the Gulf War. The Buccaneers deployed to the war zone to carry out target-designation missions carried a wealth of erotic imagery based around male fantasies – harem girls, women pirates and witches to name but a few, often

Right: *A General Dynamics F-111E of the 20th Tactical Fighter Wing which flew out of the Royal Air Force base at Upper Heyford, Oxfordshire, 'Heartbreaker' has a modern version of a World War II pin-up emblazoned along its nose.*
Below: *'Red Lady II', an F-111 bomber, carries a more restrained version of female 'nose art' featuring the head of a flame-haired temptress. Not all female artwork relies on the purely erotic depiction of women.*

dressed in stockings and suspenders or thigh-length boots. The names of girlfriends and brands of Scottish whisky also appeared on the fuselage. 'Sea Witch' carried a voluptuous female, naked except for black stockings,

Below: There can be little doubt about the war being fought by 'Desert Belle' an A-10 Warthog of the 511th Tactical Fighter Squadron. The reclining figure is surrounded by desert symbols – a stretch of sand and a palm tree.

stilettos and pointed hat, riding a broom stick. The name of a girlfriend, 'Debbie', and a whisky, 'Tamnavoulin', completed the work. Victor K.2 tankers, with names such as 'Maid Marion', 'Saucy Sal' and 'Lucky Lou', were also painted with similarly attired females. Each also carried a spear, a phallic symbol which, to put the whole thing into a rather more straight-forward and prosaic perspective, also happens to be part of 55 Squadron's official badge which features an arm brandishing a spear.

Sex objects and crude graffiti
The images of women seen on this type of 'nose art' are often accompanied by some saying, usually with an ambiguous meaning. The line 'Target for Tonight' appeared on a USAAF B-17 in World War II and could represent the obvious with regard to a bombing mission. However, the imagery of four sirens, a champagne glass and music score, suggests the altogether more alluring target of 'wine, women and song'. Similarly, the B-24 attached to the USAAF's 7th

Bombardment Group, 'Home Stretch', shows a blonde struggling to remove her underclothes. More recently, a B-52 of the 416th Bombardment Wing had a re-creation of an *Esquire* gatefold of a yawning, stretching woman dressed in a tight crimson dress. Its name, 'SAC Time', was a clever play on words: 'Sack', the slang for bed, and 'SAC' standing for Strategic Air Command, the unit's umbrella organisation.

Much of the graffiti that accompanied female 'nose art' was, however, usually somewhat cruder than the above examples, though the offending words were often run together to disguise their sexual content. 'Freenesi' (pronounced 'Free 'n' Easy') was an Eighth Air Force B-17 and 'Miss Minooki' ('Miss My Nookie'), a B-29 Superfortress, were just two examples among many, but the most popular example of the genre was – and is – 'Lakanookie' ('Like Nookie?'). Although the spelling has varied down the decades, the saying has been spotted on B-24s and B-17s in World War II and, more recently, on the A-10 tank-buster 'Lakanuki' of the USAF's 511th Tactical Fighter Squadron (see page 49).

It is not the case, however, that all women portrayed on the sides of aircraft are seen as

Below: The seer on the A-10 'The Fortune' reveals the future for anyone unfortunate enough to be on the receiving end of the aircraft's awesome array of anti-armour weaponry. The Warthog flies with the 23rd Tactical Fighter Wing.

purely sex objects, or that the accompanying graffiti is sexual. In some cases, the artwork represented a crew's or squadron's genuine affection for a particular woman. 'Lady Helen of

Below: *A Royal Air Force Tornado GR 1, 'Donna Ewin', has an impressive mission tally. The aircraft also carries the acronym TIALD indicating that it was hurriedly equipped with a new Thermal Imaging and Laser Designation pod.*

Wimpole', a USAAF B-17 Flying Fortress with the Eighth Air Force's 91st Bombardment Group, carried a faithful rendition of the said woman's face on the forward fuselage, as did a second 91st Group Fortress, 'Our Bridget'. A third Fortress, flying with the Ninth Air Force's 385th Bombardment Group, was named 'Ruby's Raiders' after Corporal Ruby Newell of Longbeach, California. Newell worked with the 3rd Bomb Division and had been chosen as the

most attractive member of the Woman's Air Corps in the European Theatre of Operations by *Stars and Stripes* magazine. Other aircraft might commemorate a woman who had died in battle. 'In Memory of Lt. F. Slanger U.S.A.N.C.' was a P-38 of the 367th Fighter Group which carried an image of the woman who had been a member of the United States Army Nursing Corps.

Inspiration for the female artwork that appears on aircraft has also come from the film

Right: 'Nikki', complete with said woman in revealing orange-red dressing gown, returns to home base with a total of 18 sorties including four laser-guided bomb missions.

Below right: 'Armoured Charmer', a Tornado GR 1, returns to England at the end of the war in the Gulf. This aircraft was one of five in the conflict that carried the TIALD system. The impossibly fulsome blonde in the tight-fitting green dress offers an erotic pout to the camera.

Above: *Exotic lingerie plays an important part in much female 'nose art', reflecting the standard theme of 'woman-as-sex-object'. The addition of an ammunition belt on her upper thigh reinforces the stereotypical image on this Royal Air Force Tornado.*
Left: *'I Luv Gaynor', a Gulf War Tornado – another example of the graphic art of the usually restrained British – shows off the overtly phallic nature of much female artwork. The laser-guided bomb would have given Freud a psychoanalytical field day.*

business. As previously mentioned, Betty Grable was a popular choice, but she was also joined by a host of other stars and their characters. Vivien Leigh, who featured in the blockbusting movie 'Gone With the Wind', provided the name – if not the inspiration for the 'nose art' – for 'Scarlett O'Hara', a B-17 of the 379th Bombardment Group, while Marlene Dietrich provided both the name and figure for 'Marlene', an unidentified B-24. Aircraft named 'The Sweater Girl' usually carried an image of actress Lana Turner as that was her nickname. The Canadians also got in on the act with a Liberator from 159 Squadron, 'Lady X', which had a superb full-figure portrait of actress Margaret Lockwood splashed across its nose.

Above: *Probably the most expertly executed artwork in the Gulf appeared on the Victor long-range tankers of the RAF's 55 Squadron. Apart from the posing 'Maid Marian', this example has a secondary image painted onto the forward cabin door with the graffiti 'I ran offut'.*

Right: *The teasing image of a French maid wearing short skirt, tight black dress and stockings as rendered on the fuselage of a Royal Air Force Jaguar – but with blonde hair?*

Flying high with 'Lili Marlene'

Images of women have also been used to accompany famous songs of the day on aircraft. In World War II, for example, 'Pistol Packin' Mama', a popular hit that was heard around the world, spawned many examples of 'nose art' which invariably featured a suitably dressed and armed cowgirl. Glen Miller's 'In the Mood' was also favoured by artists, appearing on at least one P-47 in the war and, more recently, on an F-16. One B-24 featured a picture of 'Lili Marlene' bathed in gaslight waiting by the barrack gate just as she did in possibly the most famous song of the entire war. In the Gulf campaign, a US Navy EA-6B Prowler was given the name 'Eve of Destruction' after the hit single by Barry

Left: One of the most photographed pieces of Gulf War art appeared on the Jaguar 'Mary Rose'. Executed by Chris Froome, it comprises a long-legged beauty dressed in underwear and billowing black cloak. The other side of the aircraft was decorated with a white rose.

Top: A multiplicity of images can be identified on this Buccaneer – a harem girl (rather bizarrely dressed in stockings and suspenders), two types of alcohol (Guinness and whiskey) and a woman's name. All, presumably, things missed in the Gulf. **Above:** More of the same on the Buccaneer 'Jaws'.

Above: 'Lucky Lou' peers apprehensively from her position on the forward fuselage of a Victor tanker. The slip-stream produced by high-speed flight has obviously had a detrimental effect on her hair and clothing!

Left: Drinks are served in this very slight variation on a well-worn female theme painted onto the side of the RAF Jaguar 'Diplomatic Service'. The aircraft, despite its unwarlike name, has an outstanding tally of missions to its credit.

McGuire. The artwork was a 'classic' of its type as it also featured 'Deception Lass', a curved blonde riding a HARM anti-radiation missile.

Male pin-ups go to war?

Women, then, are the most common, popular and widely appreciated form of 'nose art'. The

Above: 'The Fying Mermaid', a Buccaneer, has a variety of mission markings to its credit. The red bomb represents ordnance dropped by the aircraft; those in black indicate target-illumination sorties for other aircraft. The scorecard also includes an Iraqi Antonov An-12 'Cub' aircraft.
Right: The source of the art on the Buccaneer 'Sea Witch' was allegedly the artist's girlfriend.

portrayal of women as manipulated playthings is, in modern terms, considered cheap and unacceptable. This is probably true; certainly the images were – and are – exploitative, unrealistic and clichéd. Generally they represent woman in the time-honoured fashion of virgin-whore, saint-sinner, victim-avenging angel. But this is neither unusual or, necessarily, unacceptable given the fact that they are the product of a totally artificial environment that is populated by young, often sexually immature men. Certainly, the images portrayed in wartime on aircraft are different from those shown in peacetime, but herein lies the key and most problematic issue.

War engenders an entirely different morality – though some would say there is a total lack of morality – to that which exists in everyday life and, whether it is acceptable or not, it cannot be judged outside of that context. The other question that remains to be answered is whether or not men would find it acceptable to see stereotypical images of themselves – blonde, blue-eyed and bulging with muscles or dressed as a 'toy boy' – on aircraft. Given the fact that increasing numbers of women now serve with air forces around the world – and many are being trained for frontline combat roles – it is a question that male service personnel will have to address sooner rather than later. But even this is a matter of debate: is it a question of equality of choice or corruption, presupposing women would want to paint their aircraft as men do? Only the exponents of 'nose art' in the future – and their societies – will be able to judge.

HEROES AND VILLAINS

Pilots and aircrews have always painted images of heroes and villains, along with good luck charms, on the fuselages of aircraft. Their inspiration is drawn from many sources – historical and mythical figures, symbols of good and evil – but often represent rival war leaders.

One of the most widespread and diverse forms of 'nose art' is the representation of heroes and villains, invariably with the former overcoming the latter in someway. These images are sometimes historical in nature, but, more often than not, they are likely to depict characters – usually war leaders – directly involved in the conflict. The images created by the artists cover the whole gamut of aircraft art and range from simple complimentary or derogatory graffiti to larger images of 'good' ('our side') triumphing over 'evil' ('their side').

Little of this type of art occurred in World War I, though a few examples were known, often carrying symbolic representations of warring countries. Otto Fuchs' Albatross fighter carried a cockerel (France) being chased by a fox ('Fuchs' is German for fox); an American pilot, Major Boots, flew the Curtiss JN-4H 'Boots to the Kaiser' which featured a large boot (obviously a pun on the pilot's name) being applied with considerable force to the posterior of a caricature of the German emperor. The image of an opposing war leader being given the boot has remained a popular theme down to the present.

Enter the 'Boche Buster'

World War II, however, saw many more examples of this type of art, featuring many of the war's political and military leaders. Not surprisingly, Hitler and Nazi Germany in general were common subjects on Allied aircraft during the period. Examples ranged from simple slogans such as 'Boche Buster', a B-17 Flying Flying Fortress attached to the USAAF's 401st Bombardment Group, to more elaborate artwork of the type that appeared on the B-17 'E-RAT-ICATOR' which flew with the Eighth Air Force's 452nd Bombardment Group. The image accompanying the name comprised a cringing rat with the head of Adolf Hitler trying in vain to dodge a bomb labelled 'Rat Poison'. The Royal Canadian Air Force also got in on the act with a Vickers Ventura which featured Adolf Hitler attempting to juggle several balls labelled 'Poland', 'Norway', 'France' and 'Russia'. The

Left: An excellent example of modern 'nose art' appears on this 42nd Bombardment Wing B-52G 'Eternal Guardian'. The design – 'Old Glory' and a hybrid eagle/gryphon holding a bomb – obviously reflects SAC's role within US defence policy.

Below: *A typical piece of swashbuckling artwork is visible on the cowling of this US Navy Vought F4U Corsair as it banks to port. Emblems with a piratical flavour, particularly the 'Jolly Roger' (skull and crossbones) flag, have always been a popular motif with fighter pilots.*

Bottom: *This later version of the Corsair carries another example of the genre – a skull with a black patch over the right eye and a flowing red bandana worn around the head.*

Below right: *An obvious, but beautifully executed, death's head adorns the nose of the P-40 'Burma'.*

latter ball had crashed down onto the dictator's head implying, correctly, that he had bitten off more than he could chew when he turned eastwards in the summer of 1941. One of the finest examples of this type of art appeared on a B-17 attached to the 388th Bombardment Group's 563rd Squadron. 'Lightning Strikes' had the infamous dictator fleeing an outside wooden shack where he had been answering a 'call of nature' at the precise moment that a bolt of lightning was striking its roof. Clever touches included Hitler holding up his pants with one

hand and a left shoe that had a hole in its sole. Occasionally, aircrews might commission a piece of artwork which reflected their anger against a whole nation rather than its leader. The B-17 'You've had it!' received an extensive piece of art that consisted of a map of Nazi Germany. A large bomb was then positioned directly over the capital Berlin, which was obscured by a massive explosion. Obviously, the crew had great expectations, not entirely correct as it turned out, that the Allies' strategic bombing campaign would bring the Third Reich to its knees.

Other theatres of war carried similar examples of this form of 'nose art'. 'Miss Judy', a B-29 that flew from the Mariana Islands in the Pacific with the 462nd Bombardment Group, wore a superb piece of nose art. 'Miss Judy', a blonde, was smashing a bespectacled General Hideki Tojo, Japan's prime minister, over the head with a sledgehammer; Tojo was sinking beneath the surface accompanied by the traditional Japanese 'rising' sun. The B-29 reached Tinian in the Marianas in June 1945 to prepare for missions against the Japanese home islands, by which time the writing was on the wall for the Japanese (interestingly, Tojo resigned his government post after accepting responsibility for the fall of the Marianas in the summer of 1944). Other examples of the genre produced considerably less complex artwork. 'Finito Benito – Next Hirohito', a North American B-25 Mitchell bomber, had no caricatured art of its subjects, but nevertheless summed up the mood of the Allies following the execution of Italian dictator Benito Mussolini in April 1945. By this stage the war in Europe was virtually over, only Japan, under the nominal leadership of Emperor Hirohito, remained to be dealt with. The B-24 Liberator '12 Targets to Tokyo' plotted the advance of the Allied forces across the central Pacific. The collapse of the Japanese Empire under the onslaught was graphically illustrated by a series of explosions that corresponded to islands recaptured during the ground offensive, including Tarawa, Makin, Kwajalein and Truk. To reinforce the argument that Japan's days were numbered, a B-24 was pictured heading for the enemy's home islands.

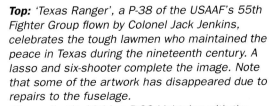

Top: 'Texas Ranger', a P-38 of the USAAF's 55th Fighter Group flown by Colonel Jack Jenkins, celebrates the tough lawmen who maintained the peace in Texas during the nineteenth century. A lasso and six-shooter complete the image. Note that some of the artwork has disappeared due to repairs to the fuselage.
Above: 'Lucky Irish', a P-38 Lightning with the 367th Fighter Group's 392nd Squadron, was flown by Lieutenant Gerald O'Donnell until he was forced to bale out over Holland in August 1944.

Other aircraft in the war featured contemporary national heroes; these could be leading politicians and statesman, media figures in general or wartime heroes. One of the most famous examples of this type of 'nose art' was the B-17 'General "Ike" '. The creator of the 'Memphis Belle' artwork, Anthony Starcer of the 91st Bombardment Group, was responsible for the design which featured a portrait of General Dwight D. Eisenhower, the Supreme Commander of the Allied Expeditionary Force in Western Europe, with a line of four stars that reflected his rank of senior general.

Most conflicts have spawned this form of 'nose art', and the 1991 Gulf War was no exception. Several aircraft from the Coalition forces carried often crude images of the Iraqi leader and instigator of the conflict, Saddam

Right: The B-29 'Miss Judy' features the said woman taking a sledgehammer to the head of the Japanese war leader, General Hideki Tojo. The aircraft flew with the 462nd Bombardment Wing.

Above, far left: Film star Clarke Gable admires the stereotyped image of a Southern gentleman of the Civil War era on the fuselage of the B-17 'Delta Rebel No.2'. This bomber, part of the 91st Bombardment Group, was lost on 12 August 1942 during a mission to Gelsenkirchen.

Above centre: A lucky escape for the B-17 'Duke of Paducah'. On 30 December 1943, the nose of this 91st Bombardment Group aircraft was hit by the wing of a second Flying Fortress. Paducah is a town in the American state of Kentucky.

Above right: The commanding officer of the 91st Bombardment Group's 324th Squadron, Major Aycock, poses in front of the B-17 'Desperate Journey'. Clearly, Adolf Hitler, the villain of the piece, is getting his comeuppance at the hands of an avenging American eagle.

Right: A portrait of an all-American hero appears on 'General "Ike"', a Flying Fortress with the Eighth Air Force's 91st Bombardment Group. Eisenhower, a four-star general, was made Supreme Commander of the Allied Expeditionary Force in Western Europe in December 1943.

Top: A B-17 from the film 'Memphis Belle' carries a skit on the baseball player Babe Ruth. 'Baby Ruth' is dressed in semi-military kit (with diapers) and shoulders a baseball bat.

Above: Halifax III 'Friday the 13th' served with the RAF's 158 Squadron. Aside from the piratical grim-reaper image, the aircraft also wore various awards, a crown and a horseshoe.

Left: A B-25 Mitchell with native American motif.

Hussein. One Royal Air Force Jaguar showed Saddam Hussein's backside on the receiving end of a sizeable boot, out of which flowed a billowing Union Jack. A USAF A-10 Warthog also carried a similar artwork that saw Saddam Hussein 'heading for the hills' on a galloping camel pursued by a homing missile; the accompanying graffiti was short and to the point – 'Holy *-...+!'. A US Navy A-7 Corsair flying off the carrier *John F. Kennedy* carried an altogether simpler message: 'Desert Storm'.

The Alamo takes to the skies

While some aircraft have carried symbols that ridicule or denigrate the enemy, others have celebrated allied forces and their leaders. Soviet leader Joseph Stalin appeared on several British aircraft in World War II, for example. In the Gulf some aircraft wore symbols that represented all or some of the members of the Coalition against Iraq. One A-10 from the 511th Tactical Fighter Squadron, 'Brothers in Arms', received an artwork that contained the national flags of the leading allied forces: the United States, the United Kingdom, France, Italy and Egypt, among others. 'Arabella II' from the same unit was adorned with two outlines: the United States picked out in the 'Stars and Stripes', and a white outline of Great Britain pictured against a vivid background of the Union Jack.

Although villains are seen on many aircraft during times of war, heroes, both male and female, real and imaginary, are also well-represented. Heroes and heroines can be taken from many spheres of life. In the case of the United States this can involve many characters, though given the history of the Wild West with its gun-toting sheriffs and robbers, Red Indians

Above left: USAF F-16C 'Gunman', adorned with a long-barrelled Colt revolver, captures the spirit of the Wild West and the gung-ho attitude of the best pilots, the so-called 'Top Guns'.
Above right: 'Honest Entry', a civilian racer, captures the skill of the early aviators. Other symbols include a balloon and a Japanese aircraft.
Right: An image of freedom American-style, as created on the fuselage of the F-111 'Miss Liberty', comprises the famous Statue of Liberty and a version of the 'Stars and Stripes' that has more than just a passing resemblance to a missile or bomb of some description.
Below right: Native Americans, usually in their full war panoply, remain a popular form of 'nose art'. This example, 'The Chief', is an F-111.
Below: Art on a Swiss Air Force Pilatus P-2 depicts a pilot with winged headgear and a pair of fangs protruding from a glum-looking mouth.

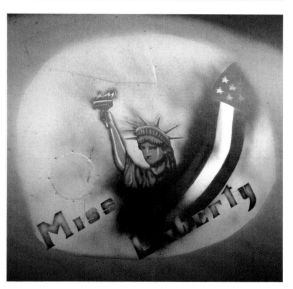

Above: *A fine example of an American cartoon superhero, dressed in a Superman-type costume in dark blue, red and yellow, appears on this F-4 Phantom which flew with VMFA-321.*

Left: *'Out of the North', a 42nd Bombardment Wing KC-135R, pictured in England during 1989. Artwork includes a Viking hero type and, bizarrely, a can of Australian lager!*

Below left: *Symbols of death and destruction are often plundered for use as 'nose art'. This Sikorsky CH-53C is named 'Headhunter' and is decorated with a gaping-mouthed skull impaled on a sharpened stake.*

Below: *Shades of Britain's most famous warrior queen appear on this Lynx helicopter stationed at HMS Campeltown. Boadicea led an ill-fated uprising against the Roman Empire in AD 62. The scythed chariot was something of a trademark!*

and cavalry, it is these that seem to dominate aircraft 'nose art'. During the 1939-45 conflict, several USAAF fighters carried gun-slinger motifs including the Lockheed P-38 Lightning flown by Colonel Jack Jenkins of the 55th Fighter Group. The aircraft was named 'Texas Ranger' after the famed frontier lawmen who patrolled the Lone Star state. The design of a lasso and holstered six-shooter was completed by Sergeant Robert Sand, and, unusually, the same artwork was fitted to at least three different fighters by the simple method of transferring the piece of cowling on which it was painted to the new mount as required. Other historical references might relate to actual events that had state or national significance. 'Fort Alamo II', a B-17 that fought in the Italian campaign, had a splendid representation of the famous mission in St Antonio, Texas, where a handful of Texans fought to the death against General Santa Ana's Mexican forces in early 1836.

Rebels and Yankees

Another popular historical strand that has found its way onto US aircraft is taken from the American Civil War (1861-65) and usually refers to the Confederate, or Rebel, side. Many aircraft have received such artwork. One World War II B-17 Flying Fortress of the USAAF's 91st Bombardment Group, 'Delta Rebel No.2', was adorned with a Civil War-era Southern colonel complete with a white pointed beard and elongated moustache. In this context it is likely that the word 'Delta' refers to the state of Mississippi, in which the delta of the river

Above: *KC-135 tanker 'Ultimate Warrior' flies with the 305th Air Refueling Wing out of Grissom Air Force Base, Indiana. The artwork consists of a thoughtful Indian chief.*
Above right: *This 97th Bombardment Wing B-52 carries a much fiercer chief with war bonnet.*
Right: *A very muscular 'liberty' figure holds aloft the US flag while brandishing a broad-bladed sword. 'Stormie' is a KC-135 tanker which served in Operation 'Desert Storm'.*
Far right: *A menacing clown with fangs appeared on the KC-135 'Jester' of the 1701st AREFW.*

reaches the Gulf of Mexico. A similar Southern gentleman also appeared on another 91st Group B-17, 'Rebel's Revenge', which was lost over Emden in late September 1943. The spirit of the Confederacy lives on into the present era. 'Rebel Rider', a Vought A-7 Corsair that was attached to the Virginia Air National Guard's 192nd Tactical Fighter Group, carried the full panoply of Yankee and Confederate iconography. This comprised an American eagle which grasped a bomb and cannon in its powerful talons, the Confederate flag, and a statue of a horse-mounted Southern general who was holding the Virginia state flag aloft in his left hand. A second piece of writing, 'Richmond, Virginia', rounded off the extensive ensemble. Not all aircraft were allied to the Southern cause, however. One of the 381st Bombardment Squadron's Flying Fortresses in World War II was known, somewhat contradictory, as 'Yankee Rebel'.

Native American Indians have also proved a fruitful source of images for aircraft 'nose art'.

The work generally falls into three categories: heads, full figures and cartoon-like caricatures. 'Packawalup' (Pack a Wallop), a B-17 with the Eighth Air Force's 457th Bombardment Group, featured a stony-faced Indian, while 'Wa-hoo!', a Flying Fortress attached to the Eighth's 306th Group, was covered with a much more graphic image which featured a tomahawk-armed Indian about to scalp a figure that bore a passing likeness to Adolf Hitler. More recently, USAF B-52 Stratofortresses and KC-135 tankers have carried similar images of Indian chiefs complete with traditional headdresses. Names such as 'Ultimate Warrior' or 'The Chief' were used to describe the artwork. Presumably the Indians' renowned fighting abilities, particularly their

swiftness and skilful hit-and-run raiding, made them a popular choice for 'nose art'.

It is hardly surprising that evil and all of its symbols – the devil, demons, witches and so on – are a strong force in much aircraft 'nose art'.

Many airman adopt a 'devil may care' attitude to their precarious and dangerous work that is frequently reflected in the type of art that they wish to see on their aircraft. In World War I, for example, the famous French ace Charles Nungesser had a collection of 'death' symbols painted onto the fuselage of his Nieuport fighter. These consisted of a coffin, a pair of candlesticks and a skull and crossbones, all pictured against a black heart. In the period 1939-45, aircraft of many nations carried similar motifs. One of the most renowned Royal Air Force bombers of the period, the Halifax III 'Friday the 13th' belonging to 158 Squadron, had a piece of 'nose

Left: A USAF KC-10 Extender tanker taxies along a runway. The Irish-based motif includes a leprechaun and four-leaf clovers.
Below: 'High Roller', a B-52 attached to the 416th Bombardment Wing which flies out of Griffis, New York, features two dice.
Bottom: A complex piece of heraldic artwork consisting of a gold crown, flags and a black ram with impressive horns on a KC-135 tanker.

art' that featured a skull and crossbones with the grim-reaper's scythe which was dripping blood onto the skull. To complete the grim vision, a biblical motto, 'As Ye Sow, So Shall Ye Reap', was added. To offset the symbols of ill-fortune, a lucky horseshoe was added to the work.

Gremlins, mischievous rather than outright evil, have been a highly successful genre of 'nose

Right: *The A-10 Thunderbolt II 'Brothers in Arms' of the USAF's 511th Tactical Fighter Squadron has received a specially created artwork celebrating the Coalition forces that fought in the Gulf.*
Below right: *A phoenix arising from the flames has been expertly applied to this A-10 tank-busting Warthog aircraft pictured after the end of the conflict against Iraq.*
Bottom right: *No prizes for guessing the villain being chased by a stylised guided missile pictured on this A-10 which also carries a range of 'kill' markings against tanks, armoured carriers, artillery, missile launchers, radars and soft-skinned vehicles.*
Below: *Desert Shield turns to Desert Storm in this artwork applied to an Allied long-range tanker.*

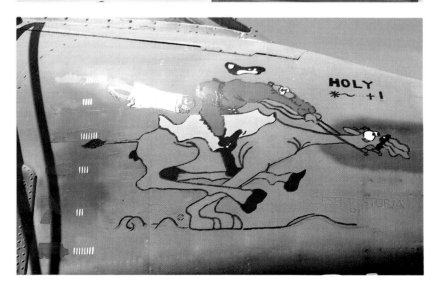

Right and below right: Saddam Hussein is on the receiving end of a large 'Union Jack' boot. The aircraft is the RAF Jaguar 'Sadman' which undertook more missions than any other British jet in the Gulf War. It unleashed nearly 100 1000lb bombs, 41 cluster bombs and 38 CVR-7 rockets during the course of the conflict.

art'. Complex pieces of machinery such as aircraft often have niggling mechanical problems that appear without any warning and often disappear equally as suddenly for no apparent reason. Aircrews and technicians like to ascribe such technical glitches to these imaginary creatures. 'Gremlin Trainer', a B-17 Flying Fortress, was accompanied into action by four of these little fellows, who had been cleverly drawn in the process of affixing a name plate to the nose of the said aircraft. One gremlin, 'Superstitious Aloysius', was particularly popular and popped up on aircraft of all types. His greatest attraction to pilots was, perhaps, the many good luck symbols that he carried on his person – a four-leafed clover, horseshoe, rabbit's foot and a wishbone.

Symbols of bad luck or macabre humour are, to a large extent, countered by a plethora of images that reflect good luck. Most of the material is fairly obvious and very much in the mould of those totems carried by 'Superstitious Aloysius', but other symbols require a little more explanation. Some are based on well-known sayings such as 'the luck of the Irish'. Many aircraft have carried art that reflects this supposed characteristic of the Celtic race and, more often than not, with a pugnacious individual living up to that other cliche of the 'fighting Irish'. Shamrocks, four-leaf clovers and leprechauns are often sprinkled about the main image to reinforce the overall message.

Uncle Sam and Britannia

National emblems are another favoured motif in 'nose art'. American aircraft have tended to carry three main symbols: Uncle Sam, the Statue of Liberty and the American eagle. All three have often been set against a backdrop of the US flag and given a suitably patriotic tag. Uncle Sam is usually portrayed as the white-haired and bearded patriarch dressed in a 'Stars and Stripes' top hat with a suitable saying. Examples abounded in World War II. For example, there was 'Yankee Doodle' (itself, a song that has strong historical implications to the people of the United States), a 97th Bombardment Group Flying Fortress that featured a grim-faced Uncle Sam grasping a large bomb. Other aircraft carried clearly identifiable motifs rather than the man himself. 'Yankee Doodle Dandy', a Flying Fortress of the 390th Bombardment Group, was decorated with the 'Stars and Stripes', top-hat

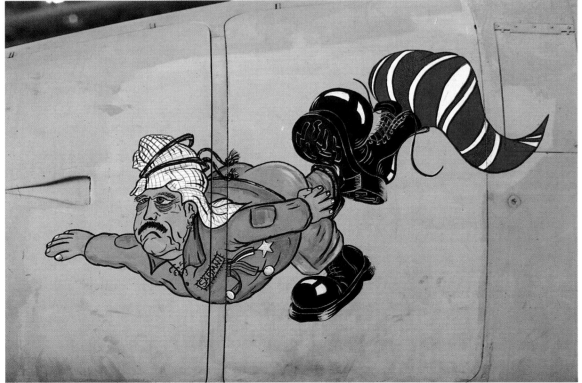

and white cane. Occasionally, Uncle Sam would undergo a sex change, though the key elements of national identity remained intact. 'Yankee Girl', for example, a B-17 Flying Fortress

attached to the Eighth Air Force's 384th Bombardment Group, had a leggy blonde who was draped across a pair of American flags doffing her 'Uncle Sam' hat.

The American eagle is another popular type of motif as it is a very warlike image in itself and is a widely recognised symbol of the United States. The emblem has been applied to US aircraft through the ages. In World War II, for example, the 91st Bombardment Group's 324th Squadron had a Flying Fortress named 'Desperate Journey' which had received an artwork that saw the American eagle captured in flight holding a terrified Adolf Hitler in its mighty talons. To make things very much more painful for the dictator, he was being gripped by the posterior. Other examples of this type of artwork included elements that suggested the role of the aircraft in question. 'Old Baldy', a Consolidated Liberator, had a hovering eagle about to drop a large red bomb. More recently, an F-4 Phantom of the USAF's 507th Tactical Fighter Group, 'Warbird', had the eagle grasping an M-16 rifle in one wing while playfully juggling a grenade in the other. A pair of bandoleers, one holding ammunition for the rifle and the other further grenades, added to the overall look of menace. One US tanker that performed in the Gulf War was 'Peacemaker' which had just the head of an eagle against a backdrop of the US flag positioned directly under the flight deck.

Royal Air Force jets in the Gulf War also carried easily recognisable national symbols. Britannia herself might not have appeared, but the Union Jack and the Cross of St George were to be seen on several aircraft. One piece of 'nose art' that was applied to a Jaguar consisted of a harem girl (meant to represent the theatre of operations) armed with a scimitar and carrying a shield which was emblazoned with the Cross of St George.

Heroes and villains, therefore, form a diverse category of 'nose art' that can reflect either the combatants or the opposing leaders in a war, or the rival countries' national heritage. Obviously, war leaders come and go, but some make the transition from temporary figureheads to national icons. Other popular strands remain the devil and all his minions, who probably reflect the black humour that war engenders, and good fortune, which needs no explanation in the context of war.

The Statue of Liberty, perhaps the most powerful image that encapsulated the feeling of the United States being the 'Home of the Free', has remained one of the most enduring heroines.

This stern-faced creation appeared on several USAF F-111s during the Gulf War, frequently in conjunction with the 'Stars and Stripes' and a map of the United States.

V

W

Y

Z

ACKNOWLEDGEMENTS

The author and publishers would like to thank Derek Bunce for the artwork, and the following individuals and agencies for providing the photographs:
AUSTIN BROWN AVIATION PICTURE LIBRARY: 1, 2-3, 4-5, 6-7, 9(top), 11, 13(top), 18(bottom), 19(bottom), 24, 25(top left), 32-33, 35, 39, 54-55, 59(top left and right), 60(top left and right), 61(bottom left), 63(bottom left), 71(left), 83(top left), 85(top), 86-87, 94-95(all 3), 95(top/Robt. F Dorr Collection), 106(top), 106-107, 107(top), 108(bottom), 109(top and bottom), 113, 124-125, 135(top right), 138(bottom right); **AVIATION PHOTOGRAPHS INTERNATIONAL**: 8, 15(centre and bottom), 17(top), 22(top right), 25(bottom), 26(top), 27(bottom), 28(bottom), 29(left), 30(top left and right), 31(top), 34, 37(top right), 38(left), 41(bottom), 42(right), 44(top), 45(all 4), 46(top right), 47(both), 48(both), 50(top), 51(both), 54(top), 55(top and bottom), 57(top left), 60(bottom), 61(bottom right), 63(top and right), 65(bottom), 66(bottom), 67(both), 69(top), 70(both), 72(top), 73(top left), 74(bottom left), 75(all 4), 80(top), 87(all 4), 88-89(both), 90(all 4), 91(bottom right), 92(top left and bottom right), 93(top right), 96(top), 97(bottom right), 98(right), 99(right), 102(top), 103(top left and right), 104(top), 110(top right), 111, 112(right), 115(bottom), 117(bottom), 122(top), 123(both), 125(top), 126(bottom), 127(both), 135(bottom left and right), 136(top and bottom right), 137(top left and right), 138(left and top right), 139(centre right), 140(top), 141(bottom left); **PATRICK BUNCE**: 54(bottom left), 56(top and bottom right), 81, 130(bottom left), 130-131; **MALCOLM ENGLISH**: 46(bottom), 49(bottom), 64(top), 65(top), 66(top), 68(both), 69(bottom), 82, 91(bottom left), 96-97, 98(left), 112(centre), 114(right), 117(top), 118, 128-129, 134(top), 135(top left), 136(centre and bottom left), 139(top); **IMPERIAL WAR MUSEUM, LONDON**: 29(right), 30(bottom), 58(top) 74(top and bottom right), 80(bottom), 102(bottom), 126(top), 140(top and bottom right); **PETER MARCH**: 9(bottom), 78(top and bottom), 125(bottom), 137(bottom left), 139(bottom right); **BOB MUNRO**: 12(top), 21, 22(left), 43(bottom), 49(top), 64(top), 92(top), 112(left), 115(top), 135(centre); **LINDSAY PEACOCK**: 37(top left), 50(bottom), 61(top), 72(centre), 97(bottom left), 116(bottom), 139(bottom left), 140(bottom); **TIM RIPLEY**: 26(bottom), 27(top), 72(bottom), 73(top right), 114(left), 119; **SALAMANDER BOOKS LTD**: 10(bottom), 10-11, 12(bottom), 14(top and bottom), 16(bottom), 17(bottom), 23(top), 25(top right), 36-37, 37(bottom left), 38(top and bottom), 40(top), 41(top), 42(top and left), 44(bottom), 57(bottom), 78-79, 103(bottom), 108(top); **TRH PICTURES**: 10(top), 13(bottom left and right), 15(top), 16(top), 18(top), 23(bottom), 31(bottom), 40(bottom), 43(top), 57(top right), 62(both), 71(top), 84, 84-85(USAF), 85(bottom/US Navy), 91(top), 92(bottom left), 93(right/USAF), 97(top/Alan Landau), 99(right/Department of Defense), 104(top/RAF Museum and bottom/RAF Museum), 105(top/Department of Defense and bottom), 107(bottom left and right), 110(top left/USAF), 116(top/Alan Landau), 122(bottom/Gus Taylor), 130(top left/R Winsdale), 132(top left and right/USAF), 133(top/USAF, bottom/RAF Museum), 134(bottom left/E Nevill); **MARK WAGNER**: 106(bottom), 110(bottom left and right).